Penguin Handbooks
Hedgerow Cookery

D1352579

Rosamond Richardson was born in Oxford and trained at
St Martin's School of Art in London. After working as a freelance
assistant to Liberty's fabric designer, she made a series of
television programmes on patchwork for the B.B.C.
She lives in the country with her daughter, a dog and a cat, and
is an enthusiastic cook. As well as writing books she also enjoys
creative needlework and designs stationery.

Cookery means . . .
the knowledge of all herbs
and fruits and balms and spices,
and all that is healing and sweet
in the fields and groves.

John Ruskin

Hedgerow Cookery

Rosamond Richardson

Illustrations by Molly Hyde

Penguin Books

Penguin Books Ltd, Harmondsworth,
Middlesex, England
Penguin Books, 625 Madison Avenue,
New York, New York 10022, U.S.A.
Penguin Books Australia Ltd, Ringwood,
Victoria, Australia
Penguin Books Canada Ltd, 2801 John Street,
Markham, Ontario, Canada L3R 1B4
Penguin Books (N.Z.) Ltd, 182–190 Wairau Road,
Auckland 10, New Zealand

First published 1980
Copyright © Rosamond Richardson, 1980

Made and printed in Great Britain by
R. Clay (The Chaucer Press) Limited, Bungay, Suffolk
Set in Monophoto Ehrhardt

For Emily

What is a weed?
A plant whose virtues have not yet been discovered.
Ralph Waldo Emerson

Contents

List of Plates

Acknowledgements

I am indebted to numerous good friends for enthusiastically sampling my experiments in hedgerow cookery and for encouraging me to write this book. I would like to thank Maggie Wilson for her support and company in the early days of exploring the countryside and for the use of her freezer. My thanks, too, to local farmers, especially Peter Unwin, for letting me pick their weeds; to Dr I.A. Evans of University College of North Wales; to Emily for making it fun; to Molly Hyde for providing invaluable botanical advice but, above all, for her beautiful illustrations; and to Jill Norman and Felicia Pheasant for all their work and help in putting the book together.

Once again I see
These hedgerows, hardly hedgerows, little lines
Of sportive wood run wild.

William Wordsworth

❧

That night, Best Beloved, they ate wild sheep roasted on the hot stones, and
flavoured with wild garlic and wild pepper; and wild duck stuffed with wild
rice and wild fenugreek and wild coriander; and marrow bones of wild oxen;
and wild cherries, and wild grenadillas.

Rudyard Kipling,
'The Cat Who Walked by Himself'

Introduction

The main thing about hedgerow cookery is that it is fun: both from the point of view of exploring the countryside with an increased awareness of what is in front of your eyes, and also because you are tasting new tastes, many of which are astonishingly rewarding. When I first lived in the country I hardly knew the difference between a stinging nettle and a deadnettle, let alone the fact that both are edible. Being an enthusiastic cook and enjoying experimenting at the stove, I soon turned my hand to cooking with the plants that grew around me in the wild. I was amazed at how tasty my first attempts were, and so also were my (at first) rather hesitant friends. I have had enormous fun learning – sometimes the hard way! – about the locations, seasons and edibility of plants completely new to me, and my young daughter is now as quick to identify them as I am. I have discovered endless culinary treats that lie hidden in the hedgerows, fields and woods, and enjoyed delicious meals from such unlikely plants as hops, sow thistle, chickweed and fat hen. The title 'Hedgerow Cookery' enjoys a degree of artistic licence, for I have included in this book wild plants that thrive in other locations than hedgerows, some garden flowers and shrubs, and seaweeds.

One great bonus of hedgerow cookery for me is the excuse to walk through peaceful, unspoiled countryside at my own pace, in my own time, exploring and discovering food plants in their natural habitat: what a world away from the bustle of shopping – and it has given a goal to a country walk. The sense of triumphant achievement as I come home laden with my unusual harvest of new fruits or vegetables to try out is unmatched – and season after season I still find it so. Not being a great devotee of the 'grow-your-own' ideal, I find that the principal advantage of hedgerow cookery is that the only time and effort involved consist of this idyllic expedition, which can hardly be said to make heavy demands on my time and energy – indeed it can be counted as pure pleasure.

I have had unanticipated triumphs and conversions at the dinner table, experimenting with these plants, and the best thing about both is that they have been occasions for laughter – even when the last laugh has been on me. It is such fun converting the sceptical and the incredulous as you offer them samphire as an hors d'œuvre, followed by fat hen crêpes with juniper potatoes and creamed chickweed, rounded off with an elderberry sorbet. Anyhow, my friends' expressions have been seen to change from tolerant cynicism to genuine enthusiasm, and many have been the requests for a second helping. So far no friendships have been sacrificed. Rather the reverse, in fact – many friends have made a spontaneous request for a 'hedgerow meal' each time they have reappeared.

Perhaps the major hesitation for most people is how to identify the plants, and there is no doubt that it takes time and experience to learn about them. To avoid the danger of picking the wrong things, this book has been beautifully illustrated with accurate botanical line drawings and paintings. Further books to help with identification are listed on page 237. There is a list of poisonous plants on page 231, of plants to be avoided on page 233, and of protected plants on page 230. It is certainly important to check and double check your plants before you eat them: although smell and taste are fairly good guides, they are not infallible, and this is particularly true in the case of wild mushrooms – some of which are poisonous and some even fatal. But here again there are excellent books on the market to help make mushroom-hunting a fascinating and rewarding hobby (see page 237).

Well over 100 wild plants are, strictly speaking, edible; but I have concentrated on those which I think produce worthwhile results. I have steered clear of the fauna of the hedgerows since I regard the snaring of hares and the shooting of rooks as falling into a different category from that of gathering wild plants. Also, there are several familiar herbs to be found in the wild and I have not given a great number of recipes for them since there are many books on herb cookery (see the Bibliography on page 237) which cover the cultivated varieties, and the recipes are generally applicable to those growing in the wild.

Of course the countryside must be treated with respect. I am not advocating stripping Britain of its wild plants and there are certain laws, written and unwritten, which must be observed. Firstly, it is an offence under the Conservation of Wild Creatures and Wild Plants Act of 1975 to dig up any plant whatever without the permission of the landowner. In the case of protected plants (see page 230), it is illegal to pick or gather even a fragment of them. Pick your food plants sparingly and mercifully – don't denude an area of any one plant, but give it a chance to re-establish its position. It is possible to upset the balance of nature by overpicking: the cowslip is a supreme example of a flower that used to be very common and is now scarce in certain localities, thanks to the cowslip-wine-makers of the past. Watch your step as you pick, too – it is easy to destroy delicate or rare plants by indiscriminate trampling. Don't pick from the verges of busy roads as they may be contaminated by exhaust fumes, and make sure that you are not trespassing on private land. Pick the plants when they are young – as they grow older they tend to become bitter; and always wash them before cooking or eating. As with any foods, don't over-indulge these exciting new tastes – highly nutritious and delicious as they are, they will be new to the digestive system.

Most of the plants that are worth eating are in fact so prolific that there is virtually no risk of their being obliterated; nettles, elder, chickweed, blackberries and fat hen have survived picking for centuries and anyone who is at all familiar with the countryside will appreciate their stamina. They survive the most consistent and methodical attempts to control them by gardeners and farmers alike. Of course, if you feel uneasy about picking them from the wild, you can grow many of these food plants yourself. There is no reason why fat hen, nettles, comfrey, alexanders and dandelions should not take their place in the vegetable garden – indeed some of them were regular features of medieval and Tudor gardens, and were eaten as vegetables as recently as early this century. It is not well known that a great number of familiar 'weeds' were imported by the Romans as vegetables – among them ground elder, borage, alexanders and the brassicas, including shepherd's purse and garlic mustard. They have been superseded by modern cultivated vegetables and have become naturalized in the wild, or have simply taken their place as common garden weeds, but many of them are close relatives of popular vegetables. For example, yellow rocket, horseradish and seakale are members of the cabbage family, and fat hen is related to spinach – and was, in fact, a staple ingredient of the diet of Neolithic man.

For generations throughout history man ate what was around him: laver sauce was eaten with mutton because both ingredients were found in the same environment. Venison and beef were cooked with wild thyme for the same reason. The Saxons preferred to eat wild birds, fish and game rather than slaughter their domestic animals which provided precious dairy produce. Their diet was in marked contrast to that of the Normans who imported the habit of eating farm animals, usually spit-roasted, with rich sauces. The Saxons, on the other hand, made stone-ground bread, ate a great deal of green salading and cooked milk puddings with barley or with oats and honey. One description of early hedgerow cookery sounds wonderfully gastronomic: crawfish with oatcakes, served with buttered watercress and followed by wild strawberries and cream.

From eating what grew around him, man moved on to farm and to cultivate the land, losing sight of some of the good things that originally tempted his appetite. It is a modern phenomenon to buy or to cultivate all that we eat: we are slaves to whatever is offered to us on the market. Old cookbooks abound with recipes for wild plants as naturally as they do for fish or game: and not for nothing. Everyone has heard of nettle soup for the simple reason that it is delicious. Nowadays we are bound by habit to what the High Street greengrocer has in his shop. Nonetheless, the hidden harvest continues: from March to November there is an enormous variety of nutritious food plants around us, free for the picking, and many freeze extremely well or make delicious preserves. They are rich in vitamins, minerals and proteins as well as offering novel and exciting tastes.

I once tried out nettle soup on a good friend for whose palate I have a great respect. He ate it with relish and then asked what it was: he was somewhat shaken by the truth, but he got his own back by calling it 'Weed Soup' and by subsequently suspecting every dish that appeared in my house of being Weed Pie or Weeds Vinaigrette. That, of course, is what it is – Weed Cookery. Well, why not? It's tasty, it's fun and it's free.

Rosamond Richardson

Hedgerow Cookery

Alexanders (PLATE I)

Spring and summer

Smyrnium olusatrum.
Umbelliferae family.
Biennial; common in hedgerows along the
coastline, especially in south-east
England.
Height: up to 6 feet/1.75 m.
Flowers (yellow) from April to June.

Originally introduced by the Romans as a culinary plant, this is now a common weed in localized coastal regions around Britain. Its name 'Smyrnium' derives from its myrrh-like smell, and it gets its common name from Alexander the Great, being a native of Macedonia, his birthplace. The young leaves and flower buds can be added to mixed or green salads, and the flowers used for savoury fritters (for the batter see page 53) – their taste is spicy, slightly peppery. Later on in the year, the seeds that appear can be ground in the same way as peppercorns and used for flavouring. The leaves, when added to béchamel sauce, give it a delicate herbal flavour. In the old days, a soup used to be made by blanching the roots and cooking them with nettles and watercress: indeed, the roots were eaten on their own as a vegetable and cooked in the same way as parsnips. Perhaps the best part of alexanders, however, is the stem.

Alexanders Asparagus

Take the young stems off the central stem before they become woody. Strip off the leaves and flower-heads and cut the leaf stems into equal lengths. Wash them and cook them in boiling, salted water for about 10 minutes or until tender. Drain well and serve on a hot plate with melted butter. Eat as you would asparagus, dipping the stems into the butter: they are as delicious in their own way and have a succulent texture which is at once crisp and soft. The taste is slightly reminiscent of artichokes.

Here is a recipe from the seventeenth century:

'*A Grand Sallet of Alexander Buds*'

⁊

(Pull the buds that appear in April and May off the sprays and discard any little leaves and stems. Wash them. The cooking will take just a few minutes.)

'Take large Alexander buds, and boil them in a fair water after they be cleaned and washed, but first let the water boil, then put them in, and being boiled, drain them on a dish bottom or in a cullender; then have boiled capers and currans, and lay them in the midst of a cleaned scoured dish, the buds parted in two with a sharp knife, and laid about upright, or one half on one side, and the other against it on the other side, so also carved lemon, scrape on sugar, and serve it with good oil and wine vinegar.'

Robert May, *The Accomplisht Cook* (London, 1685)

Alfalfa

Spring

Medicago sativa.
Leguminosae family.
Introduced perennial; found on waste
ground and road verges. Common only in
south-west England.
Height: up to 32 inches/80 cm.
Flowers (mauve) June to July.

The young shoots of alfalfa are rich in vitamins: they taste of green peas and, raw, are an appetizing addition to summer salads.

Angelica

Summer

Angelica archangelica.
Umbelliferae family.
Perennial; often found on river banks.
Height: up to 6 feet/2 m.
Flowers (yellow-green) June to August.

This angelica is a cultivar of the wild *Angelica sylvestris*; the *A. archangelica* is fleshier and therefore better for candying. The legend goes that angelica comes into flower on the feast of the Apparition of St Michael on 8 May, and it is said to be a protection from spirits and witches. The confection angelica is produced by candying the stems of this plant. The leaves can be used to make tea (see page 196).

To Candy Angelica

Pick the young stalks when they are tender and brightly coloured. Remove the leaves and soak the stalks in brine for 15 minutes (use 1 tablespoon of salt to every 2 quarts/2 litres of water). Rinse in cold water, then plunge into boiling water for 8 minutes. Drain and peel off the outer skin.

For every 1 lb/500 g stems, make a syrup with ½ pint/300 ml water and 6 oz/175 g granulated sugar. Pour the boiling syrup over the stems so as to cover them, and leave covered for 24 hours.

Day 2. Drain off the syrup into a saucepan, add 2 oz/50 g sugar for every original ½ pint/300 ml water, bring to the boil and pour over the stems.

Day 3 to 5. Repeat as Day 2.

Day 6. Drain off the syrup into a saucepan and add 3 oz/75 g sugar for every original ½ pint/300 ml water; bring to the boil and pour over the stems. Leave for 48 hours.

Day 8. Repeat as Day 6 and leave for 4 days. (It can be left for up to 3 weeks at this stage, if convenient.)

Remove the stems from the syrup and drain on a wire rack with a tray placed underneath to catch the drips. Put into a cool oven to dry off for 3 to 6 hours or overnight. Turn occasionally with a fork until they are no longer sticky. Stored between layers of waxed paper in airtight boxes, they will keep for up to a year.

Ash

Summer

Fraxinus excelsior.
Oleaceae family.
Common on chalky soil. Pinnate oblong
leaves.
Height: up to 140 feet/40 m.
Flowers (greenish-yellow clusters) April
to May.
Fruit (green, turning brownish-black)
July to October.

The ash tree used to be held sacred for its protective powers and it was believed that carrying ash keys was a protection against witchcraft. The failure of an ash key crop was thought to bode a royal death, and when one such failure occurred in 1648 it was later connected with the execution of Charles I in January 1649. The ash's reputation of being a tree with magical properties gave rise to the legend that it brings bad luck to the person who fells it.

Pickled Ash Keys

Pick the fruits of the ash in June or July when they are still young and tender. Wash them and cook in boiling water until they are soft, about 25 minutes, changing the water after the first 10 minutes. Drain and dry them, then pack them into jars, up to three quarters full. Add a few shavings of horseradish and some peppercorns to each jar. Pour over the ash keys a boiling hot mixture of cider and vinegar, well salted, and stand in a slow oven (250°F/130°C or gas mark ½) for 1 hour. Seal, and store for a few weeks before eating. They will keep indefinitely.

Barberry

Autumn

Berberis vulgaris.
Berberidaceae family.
Occasionally found in the wild along
hedgerows, but usually cultivated.
Height: up to 6 feet/2 m.
Flowers (yellow) May to June.
Fruits September to October.

This beautiful shrub, which produces long, oval, scarlet berries in the autumn, is named after St Barbara, to whom it is dedicated. It is becoming increasingly rare in the wild and is well worth cultivating in the garden. Barberries can be strewn over a joint of lamb or mutton during the last 10 minutes or so of roasting, making a refreshing contrast to the richness of the meat with their sharp flavour; or they can be made up in the following ways:

'*Barberry Tart*

'Gosfield Hall, Essex, February 5th 1805.
This is one of John Simpson's recipes.

'RECIPE.
'Sheet a tart pan with puff paste, put preserved barberries in, and crossbar it.

'*Preserved Barberries.*
'Ingredients: Barberries and preserving sugar, equal weights; a kettle of boiling water.
'Time: 24 hours to stand and then 15 minutes to boil up.
'Method: 1. Stand the fruit and preserving sugar in a stoneware jar in a pan of boiling water and keep the latter boiling till the sugar is melted and the barberries are quite soft.

'2. Take out the jar and let the fruit remain in it all night.

'3. Next day turn it into a preserving pan, and boil up for 15 minutes.

'4. Put into jars, tie, close and set them by for use.'

from *Good Things in England* by Florence White
(Jonathan Cape Ltd, 1932)

N.B. The berries can equally well be baked in the earthenware dish in a medium oven.

Alternatively, you could make a tart with barberry and pear preserve (see below).

Barberry and Pear Preserve

2 lb/1 kg sugar
1 pint/600 ml water
2 lb/1 kg barberries
2 lb/1 kg pears

Dissolve the sugar in the water over a low heat to make a syrup. Bring it to the boil and add the washed barberries, picked off their stems. Cook them until quite tender, then remove from the syrup. Peel, quarter and core the pears and cook them in the syrup until quite tender. Lift them out and mix carefully with the barberries. Boil the syrup for a further $\frac{1}{2}$ hour, put the fruit into warmed pots and cover with the syrup. Seal when cold.

Barberry Jelly

This can be made following the instructions for crab-apple jelly (see page 63). It was traditionally served with roast mutton. Another traditional English way of using barberries is found in the following recipe.

Candied Barberries

2 lb/1 kg barberries
2$\frac{1}{2}$ lb/1.25 kg sugar

Pick large, ripe berries and leave them in clusters. Melt the sugar in a heavy pan over a low heat until it reaches 232°F/112°C. Put the barberries in and boil rapidly for a minute. Remove and cool a little.

Drain the fruit on kitchen paper and leave in a warm cupboard overnight. Sprinkle with sieved icing sugar and leave for another day in the cupboard to dry. Store in an airtight jar.

Basil-Thyme

Summer

Acinos arvensis.
Labiatae family.
Native annual, quite rare, found mostly
in south-east England, on rocks or chalk.
Length: up to 8 inches/20 cm.

This is an aromatic herb and can be used for flavouring in the same ways as wild thyme (see page 197).

Beech

Spring

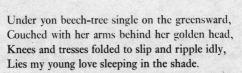

Fagus sylvatica.
Fagaceae family.
Common on very acid and alkaline soils.
Smooth grey bark; surface rooting.
Height: up to 100 feet/30 m.
Flowers (drooping clusters, creamy-
yellow) in May.
Fruits (triangular brown nuts)
September to October.

> Under yon beech-tree single on the greensward,
> Couched with her arms behind her golden head,
> Knees and tresses folded to slip and ripple idly,
> Lies my young love sleeping in the shade.

George Meredith, 'Love in the Valley'

Beech Leaves

Young beech leaves can be added raw to a green salad if they are picked very young in April or May: they are as tasty as cabbage and make an original addition to the first salads of the spring.

'English Noyau of Beech Leaves

'In a close covered jar steep as many beech leaves as the jar may hold and be covered with gin. Steep for six days, and strain off the gin (repeat if not sufficiently strongly flavoured). To every pint of gin add 1 lb sugar dissolved in about ½ pint of boiling water, and a dash of brandy. Mix, and bottle when cold. A few bitter almonds in their brown skins may be added, and some makers use more brandy. It varies locally, and seems to be a Buckinghamshire speciality. One old lady said they made it of beech *nuts* in her young days.'

Dorothy Hartley, *Food in England*
(Macdonald & Jane's, 1954)

Bellflower (Giant)

Spring

Campanula latifolia.
Campanulaceae family.
Native perennial, found in woods and
hedgebanks except in north-west
Scotland.
Height: up to 3 feet/1 m.
Flowers (blue) in June.

Apart from being a constituent of Easter ledger pudding (see page 16), the young shoots of the giant bellflower may be cooked and eaten as a green vegetable in the spring. Pick the top four leaves from each shoot, discarding any flowers, and boil them until tender, about 5 minutes. Serve with melted butter.

Bilberry (PLATE I)

(*Blueberry, Blaeberry,*
Whortleberry, Huckleberry,
Hurtleberry, Whinberry,
Wineberry)

Autumn

Vaccinium myrtillus.
Ericaceae family.
Native perennial, common on moors and
mountains. Rare in south-east England.
Height: up to 20 inches/50 cm.
Fruits (dark blue berries) July to
September.

Bilberries are delicious eaten fresh with sugar and thick cream, or made up into a crumble (see page 82) with or without the addition of apples. The leaves can be made into a tea (see page 196).

Bilberry Fritters

Wash the berries and add them to some fritter batter (see page 53). Drop tablespoons of the mixture into hot deep fat (425°F/220°C) and cook until golden brown on both sides. Drain on kitchen paper and serve sprinkled with caster sugar.

Bilberry Pie

8 oz/250 g sweet crust pastry
2 baked apples
3 oz/75 g sugar
1½ lb/750 g bilberries
milk or beaten egg

Line a greased 10-inch/25-cm flan dish with half the pastry rolled out thinly. Scoop the flesh from the baked apples and cover the pastry with it. Sprinkle with half of the sugar, strew the washed bilberries on top and sprinkle with the remaining sugar. Cover with the rest of the pastry and press the moistened edges together with a fork. Brush with milk or beaten egg and bake at 350°F/180°C or gas mark 4 for 30 minutes, or until golden. Eat it hot with cream. Serves 6.

Bilberry Cake
✳

More like a pudding than a cake, this is best served while it is still warm, with lashings of thick cream.

> 2 oz/50 g butter
> 4 oz/125 g sugar
> 1 egg, separated
> ½ pint/300 ml milk
> a pinch of salt
> 12 oz/350 g bilberries
> 6 oz/175 g self-raising flour

Beat the butter and the sugar and beat in the egg yolk, milk, pinch of salt, fruit and flour. Whisk the egg white stiffly and fold it in. Bake in a shallow tin at 375°F/190°C or gas mark 5 for 25 minutes. Serves 8.

Bilberries can be made into jam in the same way as japonica fruits (see page 116), and it's worth trying bilberry and rhubarb jam, using equal quantities of fruit and using the same method.

Bilberry Sauce
✳

> 2 pints/1.2 litres bilberries
> 1 glass red wine
> 5 cloves
> stick cinnamon
> 1 lb/500 g sugar

Bring all the ingredients to the boil and simmer for 30 minutes. Strain and put the berries to one side. Reduce the juice to a thick syrup and pour over the berries. Pot and seal. Serve with cold meats. Stored in a cool place, it will keep for up to 3 months.

Bilberry Wine

This is said by some to be the best of the country wines made from a native berry – and one of its common names is wineberry.

For 1 gallon wine:

3lb/1.5 kg berries
2½ lb/1.25 kg sugar
2 tsps lemon juice
¾ oz/20 g fresh baker's yeast,
    or 3 heaped tsps dried yeast
2 quarts/2 litres water

Make the wine following the instructions on page 221, allowing it 4 days to ferment on the pulp (see page 222, note 3).

Birch (Downy)

Spring

Betula pubescens.
Betulaceae family.
Native, hardy, found on poor sandy and
boggy soil.
Height: up to 70 feet/21 m.
White bark, peeling in papery layers.
Oval, pointed, toothed leaves.
Fruit: small winged nut in autumn, and
catkins which mature in the spring.

Birch Shoot Salad

4 oz/100 g birch shoots, the 4 top
   leaves picked when young
1 medium lettuce
1 hard-boiled egg

Wash and dry the shoots. Cut the lettuce into strips. Make a vinaigrette
with:

2 tbsps wine vinegar
8 tbsps walnut oil
1 tbsp mustard
2 tbsps chopped parsley
salt, pepper and garlic

Toss the salad in the vinaigrette and garnish with the sieved yolk and
chopped white of the egg. Serves 3 to 4.

Birch Beer

'Ingredients – ½ a lb of black birch bark, 1 oz of hops, ¼ of a lb of pimento, ¼
of a lb of ginger, 6 pints of golden syrup, ½ a pint of yeast.

'Method – Boil the bark in 3 or 4 pints of water and, when considerably reduced, strain and boil rapidly until the liquor is as thick as treacle. Meanwhile boil the hops, pimento and ginger in 6 quarts of water for 20 minutes, then strain it on to the bark extract. Stir until it boils, add the golden syrup and, when quite dissolved, strain the whole into a cask. Add 10 gallons of water previously boiled and allowed to cool, and as soon as it becomes lukewarm stir in the liquid yeast. Let it remain loosely bunged for 2 or 3 days, or until fermentation has ceased, then strain into small bottles, cork them tightly, and store in a cool place.'

From *Mrs Beeton's Household Management*, 1924

Bistort

(*Easter Ledges,
Easter Mentgions,
Poor Man's Cabbage*)

Spring

Polygonum bistorta.
Polygonaceae family.
*Perennial, common in Lancashire, less so
elsewhere.*
Height: up to 8 inches/20 cm.
Flowers (pink) May to August.

This beautiful plant is featured on the great Unicorn Tapestries in The Cloisters in New York, its delicate pink flower touching the foreleg of the captured white unicorn. Traditionally it was believed to aid conception and in the north country there is a custom that Easter ledger pudding, which contains bistort, should be eaten during the last two weeks of Lent by ladies who aspire to motherhood. It was also called 'best birth pudding' and here is a recipe for it from Kendal:

'Herb Pudding

꙳

'As made in springtime in Staveley Village, near Kendal, Westmoreland.

'Ingredients – Any kinds of edible young green herbs (wild ones) principally Easter Ledges . . ., young nettle tops, dandelion leaves, lady's mantle (alchemilla) etc. Hard boiled egg, 1. Raw egg, 1. Butter ½ oz. Pepper and salt.

'Time – To cook 30 or 40 minutes.

'Method –   1. Wash the leaves (several handfuls).
2. Put into boiling water and boil for 10 minutes.
3. Strain.
4. Chop up the leaves.
5. Add one hard boiled egg chopped up small.
6. Add one raw egg beaten up.
7. Add a little butter, pepper and salt.
8. Mix all together.
9. Put back into the saucepan. Heat through, then
10. Turn into a hot pudding basin to shape it.
11. Turn out and serve with the meat.'

Florence White, *Good Things in England*
(Jonathan Cape Ltd, 1932)

She also quotes the following extract, from *The Beauties of England and Wales* (1814), in the same book: 'Garden vegetables, except onion and a few savoury herbs used in broth were little known; but a mess made of the tender leaves of the alpine bistort (*Viparum polygonum*) called here Easter ment-gions, i.e. the sprout of the Easter month because it made its appearance about that season. Groats are the kernels of oats, divested of the inner and outer husk, and groats mixed with a small portion of young nettles, the leaves of the giant bellflower, and a few blades of chives, all boiled together in a linen bag with the meat, was accounted a great delicacy to eat with veal in the spring.'

Bistort leaves can also be used raw in salads, or blanched in soups and stuffings.

Bittercresses

Summer

Cruciferae family

Hairy Bittercress
Cardamine hirsuta.
*Common native annual, found on bare
rocks, scree and wasteland.
Height: up to 8 inches/20 cm.
White flowers.*

Hairy Bittercress

Large Bittercress
Cardamine amara.
*Native perennial, scattered in south-west
England, the Midlands and south
Scotland, in wet places and woods.
Height: up to 20 inches/50 cm.
White flowers.*

Narrow-Leaved Bittercress
Cardamine impatiens.
*Native biennial, found in woods and
damp places. Rare except in the West
Country.
Height: up to 15 inches/40 cm.
Yellow flowers from May to August.*

Wavy Bittercress
Cardamine flexuosa.
*Common annual, found on rocks and bare
ground.
Height: up to 12 inches/30 cm.
White flowers from March to September.*

Wavy Bittercress

Field Pennycress
Thlaspi arvense.
Native annual, common on verges, fields
and waste places.
Height: up to 20 inches/50 cm.
Flowers (white) May to July.

The bittercresses taste like watercress and can be put to the same uses. They are all members of the cabbage family and are well worth picking for their spicy flavour. Wash the leaves well and try them raw in salads and sandwiches.

Blackberry

Autumn

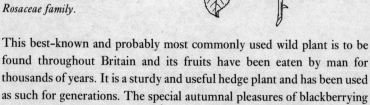

Rubus fruticosus.
Rosaceae family.

This best-known and probably most commonly used wild plant is to be found throughout Britain and its fruits have been eaten by man for thousands of years. It is a sturdy and useful hedge plant and has been used as such for generations. The special autumnal pleasures of blackberrying epitomize the general delights of exploring the hedgerows for lesser-known food plants throughout the growing year. But beware of picking blackberries after Michaelmas: folklore has it that the Devil urinates on them that night and thereafter they taste bitter.

There are classic blackberry recipes to be found in many cook books, so here are a few unusual ideas, starting with two lovely ways of making savoury blackberry preserves.

Pickled Blackberries

> 1 lb/500 g loaf sugar
> ½ pint/300 ml vinegar
> 1 tsp allspice berries
> 1 tsp cloves
> two 3-inch/7.5-cm cinnamon sticks
> 2 lb/1 kg blackberries

Dissolve the sugar in the vinegar over a gentle heat. Put the spices in a muslin bag, and put them in to simmer for several minutes. Add the blackberries and cook for between 10 and 15 minutes. Remove the spices, pack the blackberries into hot jars and then boil the vinegar down until it turns syrupy. Cover the blackberries with the vinegar, and seal the jars.

This quantity makes 4 lb/2 kg. These pickled blackberries are delicious with bread and cheese, and also make an original sweet when served with cream cheese and sugar.

A vinegar can also be made with blackberries (see page 198).

Blackberry Relish

> 1 lb/500 g blackberries
> ¼ tsp salt
> 2 oz/50 g sugar
> ¼ tsp dry mustard
> 2 cloves
> ¼ tsp cinnamon
> ¼ pint/150 ml vinegar

Simmer the blackberries in a little water until they are soft, and then liquidize them. Sieve to separate the pulp from the pips. Put with the rest of the ingredients into a pan and simmer for 10 to 15 minutes. Pour into a heated 2-lb/1-kg jar, seal and store.

This goes particularly well with ham, and also with game.

Blackberry and Chocolate Cake

3 oz/75 g butter or margarine
6 oz/175 g sugar
¼ cup blackberry jam
1 egg
6 oz/175 g self-raising flour
a pinch of salt
2 tbsps cocoa
¼ pint/150 ml milk

Cream the fat and the sugar. Warm the jam and beat it into the creamed mixture until it is light and fluffy. Add the egg and beat well. Sift the flour, salt and cocoa and add alternately with the milk. Grease and flour two 7-inch/18-cm cake tins, pour in the mixture and cook for 25 to 30 minutes at 350°F/180°C or gas mark 4.

Cool for 10 minutes on a rack. Remove from the tins and allow to cool completely. Sandwich the layers with blackberry jam and cover with chocolate icing.

Blackberries with Red Wine

Heat the berries in a pan until the juice runs, add sugar to taste and serve with red wine poured over.

Blackberry Bombe

¾ pint/450 ml blackberry purée (see below)
¼ pint/150 ml double cream
6 large meringues, broken into small pieces
¼ pint/150 ml single cream

To make the purée: Put 1 lb/500 g blackberries in the blender with a little sugar, and liquidize. Sieve to separate the pulp from the pips and sweeten to taste. This amount will make 1 pint/600 ml purée.

Whip the double cream and fold into the purée with the meringue pieces, so that it looks like marble. Put into a container, cover and freeze. Serve with extra blackberry purée and single cream. Serves 4.

Blackberry Ice Cream

$\frac{1}{4}$ pint/150 ml double cream
$1\frac{1}{2}$ oz/40 g icing sugar
$\frac{1}{2}$ pint/300 ml blackberry purée (see above)
2 egg whites
a pinch of salt

Whip the cream with the sieved icing sugar until it is thick, and fold into the blackberry purée. Beat the egg whites with a pinch of salt until they are very stiff and fold into the mixture. Put into a container, cover and freeze.

This ice cream makes excellent filling for the cob-nut meringue basket (see page 50), and is also very good served unfrozen but chilled in glasses. A lovely water ice can be made with blackberries following the method for cloudberry sorbet on page 46.

Baked Apples Stuffed with Blackberries

Hollow out large cooking apples and fill them with blackberries, well pressed down. Arrange them in a dish, pour golden syrup over them and dot with butter. Bake at 350°F/180°C or gas mark 4 for $\frac{1}{2}$ hour or until the apples are soft. Serve hot with cream.

Encased in sweet crust pastry, and brushed with beaten egg, these make extra-special apple dumplings.

Blackberry Syrup
✴

To serve with vanilla ice cream.

> 4 lb/2 kg blackberries
> 1 pint/600 ml water
> 6 oz/175 g loaf sugar per 1 pint/600 ml
>   juice

Put the blackberries in a pan with the water. Bring to the boil and simmer for 45 minutes. Strain through a jelly bag, then put the juice into a clean pan and simmer gently for 10 minutes. Remove from the heat, add the sugar and stir until it has dissolved. Return to the heat and simmer for 20 minutes. Skim, and bottle in sterilized jars.

This syrup stores well and makes a special winter treat long after the blackberry season is over.

Of course a wide variety of jellies can be made with blackberries: following the instructions for crab-apple jelly on page 63, you can make several different kinds for your store-cupboard. Here are some suggestions:

1. Add a scented geranium leaf to the fruit while it is cooking and it will give the jelly a wonderful fragrance.

2. To 1 lb/500 g blackberries add ½ lb/250 g japonica fruits and cook with water to cover.

3. To 2 lb/1 kg blackberries add 1 lb/500 g sloes and cook with water to cover.

4. To 2 lb/1 kg blackberries add 1 lb/500 g cooking apples and ½ pint/300 ml water.

5. Make a jelly from unripe blackberries.

Blackberry Cheese
✴

It seems such a shame to throw away the blackberry pulp left in the jelly bag, and this is a good way of using it.

Add enough water – about $\frac{1}{2}$ cup to every $1\frac{1}{2}$ lb/750 g pulp – to liquidize what is left. Put through the blender, then press the pulp through a sieve to separate out the pips. Measure, and add $\frac{1}{2}$ lb/250 g sugar to each 1 pint/600 ml pulp. Dissolve over a low heat and cook gently for 10 to 15 minutes until the mixture is thick. Pot and seal.

Blackberry Curd

1 lb/500 g blackberries
juice of 1 lemon
4 oz/100 g butter
$\frac{3}{4}$ lb/350 g sugar
4 eggs

Wash the blackberries and cook them over a low heat without extra water until they are soft. Sieve. Put the pulp in a bowl with the lemon juice, butter and sugar and place over simmering water until the sugar has dissolved, stirring from time to time. Beat the eggs, add to the fruit and stir over the hot water until the mixture thickens. Pot in jars and seal. Store in a cool place.

One appetizing way of using this is to spread it on dessert crêpes: roll them up and serve sprinkled with lemon juice and sugar.

Blackberry Cordial

1 lb/500 g blackberries
sugar
1 pint/600 ml sweet cider
2 tbsps honey

Liquidize the berries with a little sugar and sieve to separate the pulp from the pips. Add the cider and mix in the honey. Put in a cask for 6 months and then bottle it, straining it through muslin. Drink after 6 weeks. Makes 2 pints/1 litre. Dilute for a long drink, or serve with a dash of brandy as a liqueur.

Blackberry Cordial for Christmas
✼

> 1 quart/1 litre blackberry purée (see
> page 21)
> 1 lb/500 g sugar
> ¼ whole nutmeg
> 1 oz/25 g whole cloves
> ½ oz/15 g stick cinnamon
> 1 tbsp blackcurrant purée
> ½ pint/300 ml brandy

Cook the purée and the sugar together with the spices and the blackcurrant purée for 20 minutes. Add the brandy. Bottle and set aside for the festivities.

Blackberry Wine
✼

A good wine can be made from blackberries (see Bibliography, Books Recommended for Wine-Making, page 238).

A tea can be made from blackberry leaves (see page 196).

Borage

Summer

Borago officinalis.
Boraginaceae family.
Annual, sometimes found in the wild,
escaped from gardens.
Height: up to 20 inches/50 cm.
Flowers (cobalt blue) July to September.

Borage is traditionally added to summer drinks: the Greeks claimed that borage steeped in wine was a cure for melancholy, and Pliny was also its advocate: 'I, Borage, bring alwaies courage.' Gerard describes it in glowing terms: 'Those of our time do use the flowers in sallads to exhilerate and make the mind glad. There be also many things made of these used everywhere for the comfort of the heart, for the driving away of sorrow and increasing the joy of the mind . . . Syrup made of the floures of Borage comforteth the heart, purgeth melancholy and quieteth the phrenticke and lunaticke person.' More simply, there is an old saying, 'Borage maketh a man merry and cheerful'; and John Evelyn was even more specific: 'The sprigs of borage are of known virtue to revive the hypochondriac and cheer the hard student.' Not many herbs have received such consistent accolades from literary men!

The hairy, soft green leaves of this beautiful plant have a flavour of cucumber and make a very good filling for sandwiches. They also make delicious fritters (see method on page 53). Another suggestion is to try adding a few leaves to cabbage towards the end of the cooking time. Borage leaves added to pea soup and allowed to cook in it until soft, then liquidized, give it a subtle flavour. They can also be used to make tea (see page 196). The flowers can be candied (see page 94). One of the best recipes for borage leaves, however, is borage soup (see below).

Borage Soup

1 large bunch of borage leaves
1 oz/25 g butter
2 oz/50 g cooked rice
1 pint/600 ml chicken stock
cream
salt and pepper
borage flowers

Wash the leaves and chop them finely. Melt the butter, add the rice and heat gently, stirring well. Add the stock and bring to the boil. Put in the borage leaves and simmer for 10 minutes, then liquidize. Thin out as necessary with more stock and a little cream. Season to taste, and serve this deep green soup with a brilliant blue borage flower floating in the middle of each soup bowl. Serves 4.

'To make a tart of Borage Flowers, Marigolds or Cowslips

'This very interesting recipe comes from a "Proper Newe Booke of Cookereye", a black-letter book in the library of Corpus Christi College, Cambridge. This copy belonged to Archbishop Parker, and was edited by a Miss Frere and re-published in 1913.

'1. Take the borage flowers and parboil them tender.

'2. Then strain them and

'3. Mix them with the yolks of 3–4 eggs and sweet curds.

'4. Or else take 3–4 apples and parboil them, and strain them and mix with sweet butter and the yolks of eggs and a little mace and so bake it.'

This sixteenth-century recipe is quoted from
Good Things in England by Florence White
(Jonathan Cape Ltd, 1932)

Broom

Spring

Sarothamnus scoparius.
Leguminosae family.
Native, common on heath and wasteland.
·Height: up to 6 feet/2 m.
Flowers (yellow or red) April to June.

> Flower of the broom,
> Take away love, and our earth is a tomb.

> Robert Browning, 'Fra Lippo Lippi'

Brooms used to be made from this shrub, hence their name, and in folklore it is closely associated with the fairies. Pick the flower buds in late April or May and add them to a mixed salad. They can also be preserved. When the flowers are fully out, they can be used to make wine (for the method, see flower wines on page 222).

Pickled Broom Buds

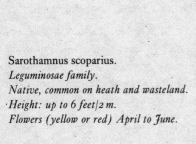

These were evidently regarded as a delicacy in the past and appeared at the coronation feast of James II. Gerard describes them in his *Herball* of 1597: '. . . The young buds of the flowers are to be gathered and laid in pickle or salt, which afterwards being washed or boiled are used for sallads as capers be and be eaten with no less delight.'

Wash and dry the young flower buds and pack them into jars. Make a spiced vinegar (see below), pour over the buds and store for a few weeks before using.

Spiced Vinegar
✵

1 quart/1 litre distilled malt vinegar
2 tbsps each of whole cloves, allspice
      berries, root ginger, stick cinnamon
      and white peppercorns

Put the vinegar and the spices into a saucepan. Cover and heat gently.
Leave on the very lowest heat possible for 2 hours. Cool and strain.

Bullace (PLATE I)

Autumn

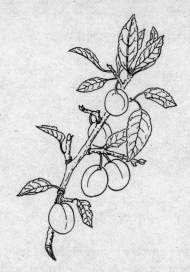

Prunus domestica, *ssp*. institia.
Rosaceae family.

This variety of wild plum flowers in the hedgerows with little white blossoms in the spring, and produces dark bluish fruits in the autumn. It is sometimes to be found in tree form in old established gardens. The fruit is larger than a sloe but smaller than the domestic plum: it makes a delicious jam and very good wine.

Bullace Jam or Cheese

bullaces
water to cover
sugar

Pick the bullaces after the first frost – they will be less bitter. Wash them and remove their stalks. Simmer them in the water until soft, then sieve them to remove the pips and skins. Weigh the pulp, and to each 1 lb/500 g pulp add 1 lb/500 g sugar. Stir over a low heat until the sugar dissolves and then boil gently to setting point. Pot and cover.

Bullace Wine

A lovely wine can be made with bullaces (see Bibliography, Books Recommended for Wine-Making, on page 238).

Burdock (Lesser)

Early summer

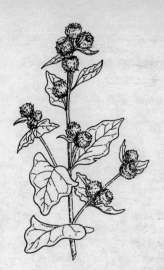

Arctium minus.
Compositae family.
Native biennial, common except in north
Scotland.
Height: up to 4 feet/1.30 m.
Flowers (purple) July to September.

Pick the young leaf stems in May and June, and peel them. Chop the cores and put them into salads, or boil them for about 10 minutes and serve with melted butter.

Butcher's Broom

Spring

Ruscus aculeatus.
Liliaceae family.
A small shrub found in woods in the south
of England.
Height: up to 2½ feet/80 cm.

Not related to broom, this handsome plant is in fact a member of the same family as asparagus. It probably got its name from the fact that its branches, with their stiff, sharp-edged leaves, were used by butchers to sweep their tables clean. One story has it that they were used for flogging chilblains! The young shoots can be boiled and eaten dipped in melted butter.

Chamomile (PLATE II)

Summer

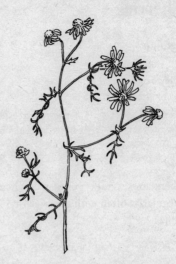

Chamaemelum nobile.
Compositae family.
Perennial, common in southern England.
Height: up to 10 inches/25 cm.
Flowers (white with yellow centres) in
June and July.

Turner, in his *Newe Herball* of 1551, says of chamomile: 'It hath floures wonderfully shynynge yellow and resemblynge the appell of an eye.'

The chopped mashed leaves of chamomile added to a cream sauce (see page 224) give it an unusual aromatic flavour which goes particularly well with fish. Chamomile leaves are also a good addition to a herb butter to serve with steak. A few leaves cooked with cabbage make a tasty difference.

Chamomile Baked Potatoes
꙯

The young leaves of chamomile can be pounded or chopped and added to softened butter – or to sour cream – and served on baked potatoes.

Chamomile Tea
꙯

Pick the flowers when they are in full bloom and dry them by hanging them in a warm place for a week or two (see Teas and Tisanes on page 196).

To make the tea, infuse 1 teaspoonful dried chamomile flowers in boiling water (1 cup) for 4 minutes. Strain it and serve. Sweeten it with honey if desired. This tea is said to aid the digestion, soothe the nerves and be a cure for insomnia.

Cherries

Autumn

Rosaceae family

> Loveliest of trees, the cherry now
> Is hung with bloom along the bough.
>
> A.E. Housman, *A Shropshire Lad*

There are several types of wild cherry growing in Britain and they fruit irregularly, often with cherries that are too bitter to be of great culinary value.

Wild Cherry (Prunus avium)

Common and widespread, this tree fruits in June with dark red cherries, usually fairly sharp-tasting. Height: up to 70 feet/20 m.

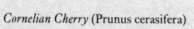

Wild
Cherry

Cornelian Cherry (Prunus cerasifera)

This variety is rare, and found only in the south of England and East Lothian. It is an ancestor of the domestic plum and its round yellow fruits can be used only if heavily sweetened in jams or pies.

Morello Cherry (Prunus cerasus)

A rare variety in the wild, with a bitter fruit that is used commercially in the production of liqueurs, and can also be made into jam.

Wild Black Cherry (Prunus serotina)

The kernels of these cherries are poisonous and it is as well to treat all types of cherry stone as such and never to eat them as nuts.

Bird Cherry (Prunus padus)

This tree produces dark, bitter fruit, pea-sized and much loved by birds. A jelly made from these cherries is known in the north as 'hackberry jelly'. It fruits from July to September and is common in the woods and hedgerows in the north and north west. Height: up to 50 feet/15 m.

Bird Cherry

Chestnut (Sweet)

(*Spanish Chestnut*)

Autumn

Castanea sativa.
Fagaceae family.
Spreading, with a broad trunk. Fairly
common in southern England.
Height: up to 100 feet/30 m.
Flowers with long greenish-yellow catkins
in June and July.
Fruits with edible brown nuts inside a
prickly green case, which holds 1 or 2
round nuts, or 3 or 4 flat ones.

The laborious process of peeling chestnuts is well-rewarded, as indeed this Italian proverb indicates: 'The chestnut is for the man who takes its shell off.' They are tasty and versatile, and as well suited to savoury as to sweet dishes.

The easiest way to peel wild chestnuts is to make a slit in the skin of each one and drop them into boiling water for a few minutes. Lift them out one at a time with a slotted spoon and peel off the outer and inner skins while still warm. Those unwilling to be peeled need to be returned to the pan for a few minutes longer.

Savoury Chestnut Dishes

1. Braise peeled chestnuts with chopped celery and a little butter in good stock until they are tender (about 45 to 50 minutes). They make a very good accompaniment to casseroled pigeon.

2. Braise peeled chestnuts in stock with a little butter, bay leaves and lean ham.

3. Braised chestnuts are delicious mixed with Brussels sprouts, especially as a side vegetable with sausages.

4. An unusual way of baking potatoes is to make a hole through the potato with an apple corer, place a chestnut in the centre and block up the hole at both ends with pieces of potato. Wrap in foil and bake as usual.

Savoury Chestnut Purée

3 lb/1.5 kg peeled chestnuts
2 stalks celery
a bouquet of herbs
stock
2 oz/50 g butter
seasoning

Cover the chestnuts, celery and herbs with the stock and simmer for 45 to 60 minutes, or until tender. Lift out the chestnuts with a slotted spoon and liquidize with a little of the stock. Add the softened butter and mix well. Season to taste.

This purée can be served as a vegetable in its own right, or used as a soufflé base. (To make the soufflé, follow the instructions for fat hen soufflé on page 92.)

Chestnut Stuffing from Grantchester

1 lb/500 g chestnuts
½ pint/300 ml milk
1 oz/25 g butter
4 oz/100 g breadcrumbs
2 oz/50 g bacon
parsley, salt, pepper and a pinch of
    sugar
1 egg, beaten

Slit the nuts and boil them for 20 minutes. Skin them, and then cook in the milk until tender. Mash with the butter, breadcrumbs, diced bacon and chopped parsley, and season to taste. Bind with the egg and use to stuff turkey or boned shoulder of lamb. It also makes a delicious stuffing for whole, braised cabbage, and, more unusually, for fish.

An alternative stuffing can be made by boiling the chestnuts until tender and then mashing them with gravy. Add an equal weight of breadcrumbs, a generous knob of butter, and season to taste with salt and pepper.

Chestnut Soup

1 lb/500 g chestnuts
1½ pints/900 ml stock
1 onion
2 stalks celery
2 oz/50 g butter
salt, mace and cayenne
cream

Peel the chestnuts (see page 34) and cook in the stock until tender. Lift out with a slotted spoon and liquidize with a little of the liquid. Thin out with more stock.

Slice the onion finely and chop the celery. Cook gently in the butter until they are soft, then add the chestnut mixture gradually, stirring well. Thin out with more stock as necessary, season to taste and finish with a little cream. Serves 4.

Chestnut Spread

5 oz/150 g cream cheese
2 to 3 tsps sour cream
½ pint/300 ml chestnut purée (see page 35)
2 tbsps grated raw chestnuts
salt and pepper
parsley

Mash the cream cheese with the sour cream. Blend with the chestnut purée and stir in the grated nuts. Season to taste and pack into jars. Spread on melba toast or crackers and sprinkle with chopped parsley and more grated nuts.

Chestnut Stuffed Eggs

For each hard-boiled egg:
1 tbsp chestnut purée (see page 35)
1 tsp vinaigrette or sour cream
salt and pepper
grated raw chestnut

Halve the eggs and mash the yolks. Add them to the chestnut purée, dress with the vinaigrette or sour cream, and season. Heap into the egg-white halves and sprinkle with grated raw chestnut.

Chestnut Pilaff

1 lb/500 g chestnuts
1 lb/500 g cooked leftover lamb
butter
water or stock
½ lb/250 g rice
salt and pepper

Boil and peel the chestnuts. Cut the lamb into cubes and toss in butter, then add the nuts and 3 cups of stock or water and bring to the boil. Add the rice and seasonings. Simmer, stirring continuously, for ½ hour until the juices are absorbed and the rice and nuts cooked. Serves 4 to 6.

Chestnut Compote

½ lb/250 g granulated or loaf sugar
18 fl oz/½ litre water
1 lb/500 g chestnuts

Dissolve the sugar in the water over a gentle heat, then bring to the boil and cook until it reaches 220°F/108°C, or until the syrup forms a thread when it runs off the spoon.

Skin the chestnuts and cook them in the syrup for 15 minutes or until tender. Chill. Serves 4.

(continued)

Made with a heavier syrup (2 oz or 50 g sugar to every 1 tablespoonful of water) and cooked until it is well-reduced, the chestnuts can be preserved in sealed jars.

Chestnut Croquettes

1 lb/500 g chestnuts
¼ pint/150 ml milk
2 oz/50 g vanilla sugar
½ pint/300 ml *crème pâtissière* (see below)
1 egg, beaten
breadcrumbs
clarified butter for frying

Peel the chestnuts and cook in the milk with the vanilla sugar until soft (about 15 minutes) or until tender. Lift out with a slotted spoon and liquidize with a little of the liquid.

Make the *crème pâtissière* and mix with the purée. Spread on a baking sheet about ½ inch/1 cm thick, and cool.

Cut into 3-inch/8-cm lengths, dip in beaten egg and breadcrumbs and fry in clarified butter (see page 225). Serve piping hot with apricot sauce (see page 50). Serves 4.

Crème Pâtissière

3 egg yolks
3 oz/75 g caster sugar
1½ oz/40 g sifted flour
½ pint/300 ml boiling milk
a knob of butter
1 tbsp vanilla extract

Beat the egg yolks and the sugar until they are thick and pale yellow. Whisk in the flour. Add the boiling milk gradually and then put in a pan over a low heat and stir until the custard thickens. Add the butter and the vanilla.

Chestnut Plombière

¾ pint/450 ml *crème pâtissière* (see
above)
¼ cup very strong black coffee
2 egg whites
12 chestnuts poached in syrup

Flavour the *crème pâtissière* with the coffee instead of with vanilla, and
while it is still hot fold in the stiffly beaten egg whites. Slice the chestnuts
and fold them into the mixture. Pile into glasses and serve chilled. Serves 6.

Sweet Chestnut Purée

1 lb/500 g chestnuts
¾ lb/350 g sugar
1 pint/600 ml water
vanilla pod

Peel the chestnuts. Make a syrup with the sugar, water and vanilla pod, and
boil the chestnuts in it until they are quite soft. Lift them out with a slotted
spoon and mash them to a purée, then mix with enough syrup to give you
the consistency you require.

This purée can be used as a base for ice cream, using the method
described for blackberry ice cream on page 21, and it can also be preserved
in sealed jars and used as a jam.

Chestnut and Cherry Ice Cream

1 oz/25 g each raisins and sultanas
1 oz/25 g each glacé cherries and
candied peel
1 small glass madeira or sherry
1 pint/600 ml double cream
4 oz/125 g chestnut purée
marrons glacés (optional)

Soak the raisins and sultanas in hot water for 1 hour, then soak with the cherries and peel in the wine. Whip the cream until it is thick and fold into the purée. Fold the fruit and the wine into the chestnut cream and put into a container. Cover and freeze. Serves 6.

Serve with whipped cream and – if you have them to spare – sprinkle with chopped *marrons glacés*.

Chestnut Topping

To serve with vanilla ice cream.

> 4 oz/100 g finely chopped, peeled
>   chestnuts
> 4 to 6 tbsps caster sugar
> 3 tbsps rose water (see page 162)
> 2 thin slices of orange peel
> ¼ tsp vanilla essence

Mix all the ingredients together and cook, stirring well, until the mixture thickens. Remove the orange peel, add more vanilla to taste, and cool.

Chestnut Gâteau

> 2 oz/50 g sugar
> 2 oz/50 g butter
> 1 lb/500 g unsweetened chestnut purée
> 3 tbsps thick syrup (see page 38)
> 2 eggs, separated

Cream the sugar and the butter, then mash in the chestnut purée, moistening the mixture with the syrup. Beat the egg yolks and add to the mixture. Beat the whites until they are very stiff and fold in gently. Pour into a greased cake tin (8 inches or 20 cm) and cook at 375°F/190°C or gas mark 5 for 1½ hours. Leave to cool in the tin, then turn out and chill.

Serve cold with thick cream as a dessert, or sprinkled with grated chocolate as a tea-time treat. Serves 8.

Chickweed (PLATE 1)

Most of the year round

Stellaria media.
Caryophyllaceae family.
A widespread and abundant annual.
Length: up to 12 inches/35 cm.
Flowers all the year round, but mostly in
the spring and autumn, with white star-
shaped flowers.

Mouse-ear chickweed: inedible

Chickweed tastes remarkably like cress and used to be sold as such on the markets in days gone by. It is a really delicious vegetable and deserves to be more widely used; of course it is so well known as a common garden weed, and so prolific, that gathering it presents no problems. It smells wonderful while it is cooking – not unlike the smell of fresh baby beetroot being boiled – but it is also very good raw in salads and sandwiches. It is particularly rich in phosphorus, potassium and iron. Don't confuse it with mouse-ear chickweed (*Cerastium fontanum*), however, as this is virtually inedible. The illustration makes clear how different they look.

To Cook Chickweed as a Vegetable

Pick a good bunch of chickweed and wash it well. Cut off the straggly roots and remove any other leaves tangled up in it. Cook, without adding extra water but with a little salt, a knob of butter and some chopped shallots or chives. Simmer gently until tender – about 8 to 10 minutes – and serve with red meat or game.

Chickweed and Lettuce Soup

1 medium lettuce
1 large bunch of chickweed
butter for cooking lettuce
   and chickweed
$1\frac{1}{2}$ oz/40 g butter
2 oz/50 g flour
$1\frac{1}{2}$ pints/900 ml stock
salt and pepper

Wash and shred the lettuce. Wash the chickweed well and cut off all the roots. Chop, and cook with the lettuce in enough butter to cook down well.

In a different pan, melt the $1\frac{1}{2}$ oz/40 g of butter, stir in the flour and gradually stir in the hot stock until the mixture thickens. Season to taste and simmer for a few minutes. Add the cooked vegetables and stir in thoroughly. Heat through and then liquidize. Adjust the seasoning and finish with the cream. Serves 4.

Alternatively, the chickweed on its own makes an admirable soup, or try making a tomato and chickweed soup.

Creamed Chickweed

Cook the chickweed (see above) and add to a generous quantity of béchamel sauce (see page 224). Heat through and serve as a side vegetable.

Chickweed Croustades

Cut bread rolls in half and hollow them out, leaving just the crusts as a shell. Fill with creamed chickweed, sprinkle with a mixture of grated cheese and breadcrumbs, dot with butter and bake at 375°F/190°C or gas mark 5 for 15 to 20 minutes.

Chickweed and Cauliflower Gratin

Lightly cook some cauliflower flowerets in boiling salted water until they are tender but not soft. Add to some creamed chickweed (see above) and mix together well. Put into a baking dish, sprinkle with a mixture of breadcrumbs and grated cheese, dot with butter and bake at 375°F/190°C or gas mark 5 for 20 minutes.

Chickweed with Cucumber

1 cucumber
butter
salt and pepper
a large bunch of chickweed
béchamel sauce (see page 224)
cream (optional)

Peel the cucumber and slice it very thinly. Melt the butter in a heavy pan and cook the cucumber, well seasoned, until it is softened. Add the washed, chopped chickweed and cook until it has wilted. Add to a generous quantity of béchamel sauce, with a little cream if you wish, adjust the seasonings and serve as a side vegetable to go with roast chicken. Serves 3.

Chickweed, Lentil and Beetroot Salad

Soak the lentils for a few hours and cook until tender in the soaking liquid. Drain, season with salt and pepper, and cool. Peel some small cooked beetroot and slice them very thinly. Wash and trim a bunch of chickweed and toss all together in a garlicky vinaigrette.

Chicory

Summer

Cichorium intybus.
Compositae family.
Common in southern England.
Height: up to 4 feet/1.2 m.
Flowers (blue) July to October.

This is, unrecognizably, the plant from which derives – by a complicated horticultural process – the chicory that we buy in the High Street.

The leaves can be used sparingly in a mixed salad, or added to a *pissenlit au lard* (see page 70).

The roots can be added to coffee to give it a characteristically bitter flavour: wash them, cut them into small pieces and dry off in a slow oven. Cut into nibs, roast again and grind before adding to ground coffee.

Chives

Summer

Allium schoenoprasum.
Liliaceae family.
Native but rarely found in the wild.
Height: up to 8 inches/20 cm.
Flowers (purple) June to July.

Well known in their cultivated form, chives are a useful and popular herb, being just as tasty raw in salads as cooked in sauces. They have a high iron content and make a good garnish for soups.

Clary (Wild) (PLATE III)

Summer

Salvia horminoides.
Labiatae family.
Native perennial, common in southern
England.
Height: up to 25 inches/65 cm.
Flowers (white and purple) May to
August.

Clary is a relative of sage and can be used, fresh or dried, in the same ways. A wine of clary and elderflowers used to be made (for wine-making instructions, see page 221). Use one third clary to two thirds elderflower.

The young leaves cooked in butter are good in omelettes, either on their own or with mixed herbs.

Clary Fritters

Dip washed, dried clary leaves into fritter batter (see page 53), and fry in deep, hot fat until golden brown on both sides. Sprinkle with sugar and a few drops of freshly pressed orange juice and serve immediately.

Cloudberry

Autumn

Rubus chamaemorus.
Rosaceae family.
Found in peat bogs and moors in the
Scottish Highlands and occasionally in
the Pennines.
Height: up to 7 inches/18 cm.
Fruits (orange) August to October.

The cloudberry can be cooked in the same way as the blackberry, and in pies and crumbles, etc. One very special and exotic dish is given below.

Cloudberry Sorbet

1½ lb/750 g cloudberries
sugar
6 oz/175 g sugar
1 pint/600 ml water
1 egg white

Liquidize the cloudberries with a little sugar and then sieve to separate the pips from the pulp. Make a syrup with the 6 oz/175 g sugar and the water by dissolving over a low heat and then boiling rapidly for 6 minutes. Cool. Stir in the cloudberry purée and freeze.

After an hour or so, when it is turning mushy, take it out and beat it with a whisk. Fold in the stiffly beaten egg white and freeze again. Serves 6.

Cob-Nut

(Hazel)

Autumn

Corylus avellana.
Corylaceae family.
Native, common.
Height: up to 20 feet/6 m.
Fruits August to November.

> Her chariot is an empty hazel-nut
> Made by the joiner squirrel or old grub.
>
> William Shakespeare, *Romeo and Juliet*

This pretty tree is said to have magical properties, and in fact hazel twigs are used as divining rods. The nuts are known as cobs, hazelnuts and filberts – the latter because the tree is dedicated to St Phillibert whose saint's day falls on 22 August, just as it comes into nut. They are extremely rich in protein and are as much sought after by squirrels as by man. Most of us have eaten cob-nuts raw, but when cooked they give a wonderful flavour to savoury and sweet dishes alike: try roasting them and see how they are transformed.

To Roast Cob-Nuts

Remove the nuts from their husks. Put them on a baking tray in a preheated oven at 350°F/180°C or gas mark 4 and cook for 10 to 15 minutes, shaking from time to time, until they are golden brown. Toss in salt while still warm, then allow them to cool.

If you can resist eating them there and then, these roasted cobs store well in airtight jars and can be used in all the following savoury recipes. For the sweet recipes, roast them as above but leave them unsalted.

Cob-Nut Butter

2 oz/50 g butter
4 oz/100 g roasted cobs

As a substitute for home-made peanut butter, this makes mouth-watering sandwiches, toasted or plain, especially with the addition of little pieces of chopped, crisped bacon.

Melt the butter and put with the nuts into the liquidizer. Blend until the butter is a nice crunchy texture, and taste to see if it needs more salt. Pack into an airtight jar and store in a cool place. It will keep for up to 3 months.

Cob-Nut Appetizer

4 oz/100 g cob-nuts
1 tsp each chopped chives, tarragon
   and parsley
2 oz/50 g butter
salt and pepper

Pound the roasted, salted cobs to a paste in a mortar and mix with the herbs. Work in the softened butter and season to taste. Spread on little cheese crackers and serve with drinks.

Cob-Nut Stuffing for Fish

2 oz/50 g diced bacon
butter
chopped fresh herbs
3 oz/75 g breadcrumbs
grated rind of ½ lemon
2 oz/50 g cobs, chopped
1 egg, beaten

Crisp the diced bacon in a hot pan with a little butter, then add the herbs until they wilt slightly. Drain off the fat and mix the bacon and herbs with the breadcrumbs and lemon rind. Add the nuts and enough egg to bind. Enough for 4 medium-sized fish.

Stuff trout or whiting with the mixture, or roll fillets of sole or plaice around it before baking in foil.

Savoury Nut Squares

1½ oz/40 g butter
1 small onion
2 oz/50 g flour
½ pint/300 ml milk
salt and pepper
2 oz/50 g breadcrumbs
2 oz/50 g ground cob-nuts
parsley
beaten egg and breadcrumbs for
    coating
vegetable oil

Melt the butter and cook the chopped onion in it until well softened. Stir in the flour and gradually add the heated milk until the sauce is smooth and very thick. Season well and add the 2 oz/50 g breadcrumbs, nuts and parsley, then spread on a tray to cool.

Cut into squares, brush with the beaten egg and dip in breadcrumbs. Fry in hot vegetable oil until crisp and golden all over.

Cob-Nut Salad

Add chopped, roasted cob-nuts to a tomato and celery salad and dress with vinaigrette.

Cob-Nut and Barley Salad

3 oz/75 g cob-nuts
6 oz/175 g barley, soaked overnight
½ pint/300 ml stock
½ lb/250 g Chinese cabbage leaves

Roast and chop the nuts as above. Drain the barley and simmer in the stock for 1½ to 2 hours. Rinse under cold running water and drain well. Shred the cabbage. Mix the nuts, cabbage and barley together and dress with a well-seasoned, garlicky vinaigrette.

Cob-Nut Meringue Basket

> 1 egg white
> pinch of salt
> 2 tbsps boiling water
> 8 oz/250 g caster sugar
> 2 oz/50 g roasted cob-nuts

Lightly beat the egg white with the salt. When frothy, beat in the water and sugar and whisk over hot water until stiff. Off the heat, beat thoroughly for another 2 minutes. Then fold in the chopped nuts.

Place tablespoons of the mixture round in a circle on a greased and floured baking tray and cook at 300°F/150°C or gas mark 2 for 1 hour. Cool on a rack. Serve with apricot sauce (see below) or fill the centre with blackberry ice cream (see page 21). Serves 6 to 8.

Apricot Sauce

> 4 oz/100 g dried apricots, soaked
>   overnight
> ½ a lemon
> 4 oz/100 g granulated sugar

Stew the apricots in the liquid that they soaked in, with a strip of lemon peel. When tender, liquidize them and then dissolve the sugar in the purée over a gentle heat, add the juice of the ½ lemon and boil for 3 minutes.

This sauce keeps for a fortnight in an airtight jar in the refrigerator.

Cob-Nut Ice Cream

> a small carton of double cream
> 1½ oz/40 g icing sugar
> 4 oz/100 g roasted cob-nuts
> ½ tsp vanilla extract
> 2 egg whites

Beat the cream with the sifted icing sugar until it is thick. Fold in the nuts and the vanilla extract. Beat the egg whites until they are stiff, then fold into the cream. Put into a container, cover and freeze. Serves 6.

Cob-Nut Tart

8 oz/250 g sweet crust pastry
2 eggs
8 oz/250 g caster sugar
1 cup chopped cob-nuts
2 tsps vanilla extract

Grease an 8-inch/20-cm flan dish and line the bottom with half the pastry, rolled out thinly.

Beat the eggs and sugar together for several minutes until very thick, then add the nuts and the vanilla.

Pour into the flan dish, cover with the remainder of the pastry and press the moistened edges firmly together with a fork. Bake at 350°F/180°C or gas mark 4 for 30 minutes. Serve cold with cream. For 6.

Cob-Nut Soufflé

2 oz/50 g butter
2 tbsps flour
1 cup hot milk
2 oz/50 g sugar
4 eggs, separated
3 oz/75 g roasted cob-nuts
1 tbsp caster sugar

Melt the butter and stir in the flour. Add the milk, stirring all the time until the sauce is thick and smooth. Off the heat, stir in the 2 oz/50 g sugar. Add the egg yolks one by one, beating with a wire whisk. Then add the nuts.

Beat the egg whites until soft peaks are formed, then add 1 tablespoon of caster sugar and beat until very stiff. Fold the whites into the base and put into a greased and sugared soufflé dish. Bake at 400°F/200°C or gas mark 6 for 25 to 30 minutes, turning the heat down to 375°F/190°C or gas mark 5 after the first 5 minutes. Serve immediately. For 4.

Cob-Nut Cookies

4 oz/100 g butter
4 oz/100 g sugar
1 egg, well beaten
1 tbsp milk
½ tsp vanilla essence
2 oz/50 g roasted chopped cob-nuts
6 oz/175 g plain flour
1 tsp baking powder
¼ tsp salt

Cream the butter with the sugar, then beat in the egg, milk and vanilla, and finally the nuts. Add the flour, baking powder and salt sifted together. Mix well and chill.

Roll tablespoons of the mixture into small balls and place on a greased baking sheet. Flatten slightly and bake at 375°F/190°C or gas mark 5 for 8 to 10 minutes. Cool on a rack.

Comfrey (PLATE 1)

Spring and summer

Symphytum officinale *(plus many varieties).*
Boraginaceae family.
Native perennial, common except in northern Scotland; found in damp hedgerows and by the sides of streams.
Height: 3 to 6 feet/1 to 2 m.
Flowers (purple or pink or white, according to the variety) May to September.

Comfrey contains all the goodness of spinach with the additional bonus of vitamin B_{12}. It is the only vegetable to contain it, so is therefore of great nutritional value to vegetarians. It has a higher protein content than any other vegetable except the soya bean and has been eaten for over 1500 years. Researchers, however, are at present looking into the action of certain alkaloids present in comfrey, so until their findings are published it would be prudent not to eat too much too frequently.

Comfrey's local name of 'boneset' derives from its extraordinary healing powers (*symphytum* means 'growing together' or 'uniting') – the root, ground and made into a poultice, was often used in the old days to mend fractured limbs.

Tea can be made from comfrey leaves (see page 196).

Comfrey Fritters

For the fritter batter:

4 oz/100 g plain flour
a pinch of salt
3 tbsps vegetable oil
$\frac{1}{4}$ pint/150 ml warm water
1 egg white

Sieve the flour and the salt and stir in the 3 tablespoons oil. Gradually add the water, stirring well until it is like a thick cream. Stand in a cool place for 2 hours and add a little water to thin out.

Beat the egg white until stiff, and fold it into the batter just before you use it.

Pick young comfrey leaves; wash and dry them well. Heat vegetable oil in a deep frying pan to 425°F/220°C. Dip the leaves in the batter so that they are well coated on either side and put into the hot fat. When the underside is golden brown and puffed, turn and cook on the other side. Drain on paper towels and sprinkle with salt.

They are delicious, and children love them too: the leaves lose their furriness in the cooking but their glutinous quality is a perfect contrast to the light, crisp batter.

To Cook Comfrey as a Vegetable

Pick the young, lighter-coloured leaves and wash them well. Cook exactly as you would spinach, in a little salted water for about 15 minutes. Drain, chop and serve with a knob of butter, and some caraway seeds if you like them, or else with croûtons. Try garnishing with chopped hard-boiled egg.

The mixture of cooked comfrey leaves and béchamel sauce (see page 224) has many uses: for example, it can be the base for a soufflé (see fat hen soufflé on page 92), and is excellent served simply as a creamed vegetable. Comfrey makes a marvellous soup when combined with nettles in equal quantities (see nettle soup on page 150).

Comfrey au Gratin

Fill a baking dish with a mixture of cooked comfrey leaves and béchamel sauce (see page 224), thoroughly stirred together. Cover with a generous layer of grated cheese mixed with an equal quantity of breadcrumbs. Dot with butter and bake at 375°F/190°C or gas mark 5 for 20 to 25 minutes.

Comfrey Pancakes

Make your pancakes in the usual way (for recipe see page 225), using ¾ pint/450 ml liquid, etc.

> 1½ lb/750 g cooked comfrey
> ¾ pint/450 ml béchamel sauce (see page 224)
> salt and pepper
> garlic (optional)
> Parmesan cheese
> butter

Cook the comfrey as above and add to the béchamel sauce, mixing together very thoroughly. Season to taste. Add garlic, if you like – it goes very well with comfrey.

When the mixture is cool, place a good spoonful in the middle of each pancake, roll it up and place in a greased baking dish. Sprinkle with Parmesan cheese, dot with butter and cook at 375°F/190°C or gas mark 5 for 25 minutes. Makes 18 pancakes.

Try using this mixture to stuff cannelloni, or as a substitute for spinach in lasagne, or in home-made ravioli.

Comfrey in Pastry Envelopes

> 3 oz/75 g each cream cheese, butter and flour
> a large pinch of salt
> 1 lb/500 g cooked comfrey (see above), mixed with
> ½ pint/300 ml béchamel sauce (see page 224)
> 1 egg yolk, beaten

Work the butter and cream cheese together until soft. Sift the flour and salt and work into the fats. Knead until light and chill for 1 hour. Roll out thinly on a floured board and cut into 5-inch/12-cm squares.

Put a large spoonful of the comfrey and béchamel mixture in the centre of each square and fold it over to make a triangle, moistening the inside edges before you press them down, to seal the pastry. Press the edges together with a fork. Brush with beaten egg yolk and cook at 425°F/220°C or gas mark 7 for 10 to 12 minutes. Serves 4.

Comfrey Puffs

2 lb/1 kg cooked comfrey leaves,
   mixed with
1 pint/600 ml béchamel sauce (see page
   224)
melted butter
Parmesan cheese

For the choux paste:
$\frac{1}{2}$ pint/300 ml water
3 oz/75 g butter
1 tsp salt
pepper and nutmeg
4 oz/100 g plain flour
4 eggs

First, make the paste. Heat the water, butter and seasonings in a thick-bottomed pan and bring it to the boil. Remove from the heat and add the sifted flour all at once. Return to the heat and stir with a wooden spoon until the paste amalgamates and leaves the sides of the pan.

Remove from the heat and add the eggs one at a time, beating very thoroughly until they are quite absorbed. Cool.

Heat the oven to 425°F/220°C or gas mark 7. Place spoonfuls of the mixture, in dollops about 2 inches/5 cm across and 1 inch/3 cm high, several inches apart on a greased baking sheet. Cook for 20 minutes and then turn the heat down to 375°F/190°C or gas mark 5 and cook for a further 15 minutes, until puffed and golden brown. Cool on a rack. Then split them open with a short cut and scoop out any soft insides.

Fill with the comfrey and béchamel mixture, brush with melted butter and sprinkle with grated Parmesan. Heat in a greased baking dish at 350°F/180°C or gas mark 4 for 20 minutes and serve immediately. For 8.

Comfrey Pie
🐦

oil pastry (see page 224), using
   6 oz/175 g flour, etc.
½ lb/250 g cooked comfrey
garlic (optional)
⅓ pint/200 ml béchamel sauce (see page
   224)
salt and pepper
2 tbsps thick cream
2 eggs

Line a greased 9-inch/22-cm pie dish with the oil pastry and bake blind.

Add the chopped cooked comfrey and optional crushed garlic to the béchamel sauce, season and add the cream. Separate the eggs, beat the yolks and add to the mixture. Beat the whites until they are stiff and fold them in. Pour into the pastry shell and bake at 375°F/190°C or gas mark 5 for 30 minutes. Serves 4.

Comfrey Salad
🐦

Add washed, shredded comfrey leaves to a green salad, perhaps with the addition of fresh herbs; dress with a good vinaigrette and you have a delicious and different salad.

Corn Salad

(*Lamb's Lettuce*)

Most of the year round

Valerianella locusta.
Valerianaceae family.
Annual, found on hedgebanks and road
verges.
Height: up to 12 inches/35 cm.
Flowers (white and purple) from April
to June.

The French word for corn salad is *mâche* and the raw leaves are eaten as a salad vegetable either on their own or else very commonly with beetroot. It leafs throughout the year and can be used in many of the recipes given for fat hen and comfrey.

It is particularly tasty in a salad of raw mushrooms and avocado, marinated for a few hours in a good garlic vinaigrette.

Cowberry

Autumn

Vaccinium vitis-idaea.
Ericaceae family.
Native evergreen shrub, common in
Scottish Highlands on moors and in
woods.
Height: up to 12 inches/30 cm.
Flowers (pink or white) May to August.
Fruits (red) August to October.

These red berries have a high vitamin C content and make an excellent jelly (for method, see crab-apple jelly on page 63).

Cow Parsley

(Queen Anne's Lace)

Spring and summer

Anthriscus sylvestris.
Umbelliferae family.
Widespread native perennial.
Height: up to 3 feet/1 m.
Flowers (white) April to June.

Cow parsley is in fact wild chervil and the leaves are much used as a herb in France. Their delicate flavour is less pronounced than that of parsley and has a slight suggestion of liquorice. They are best used freshly picked and finely chopped for salads – green or potato – or added to soups or casseroles just before serving.

Cow parsley makes a distinctive addition to an *omelette fines herbes* and gives an aromatic flavour to a béchamel sauce or to seasoned cream to serve with poached fish. It goes particularly well with hot haricot beans. Try adding the chopped leaves to softened butter and serve with baked potatoes.

Hemlock: poisonous

A word of warning: don't confuse cow parsley with its close relatives, hemlock and fool's parsley – both are poisonous (see list on page 231) so check carefully before you pick it that you have chosen the right plant.

Hemlock grows up to 6 feet/2 m tall and is distinguished by the purple blotches that appear on its stem. The stem is hollow and dangerous to touch – it can cause unpleasant lesions. The leaves of hemlock are fine and feathery. Fool's parsley, although it grows to much the same height as cow parsley, has darker cream-coloured, coarser flowers that grow in closer clusters than the white sprays of cow parsley.

Cowslip

Spring

Primula veris.
Primulaceae family.
Native perennial, found in meadows and
on banks in England and Wales,
becoming rare.
Height: up to 12 inches/30 cm.
Flowers (yellow) April and May.

> Where the bee sucks there suck I;
> In a cowslip's bell I lie.

William Shakespeare, *The Tempest*

This most English of wild flowers has become scarce through over-picking and although old cookbooks abound with recipes for cowslips – from the days no doubt when they were as abundant as cow parsley – I feel loath to include any here: given a chance the cowslip will re-establish itself – as indeed it is doing in certain localities – so perhaps it should be left alone for a while. Suffice it to say that the cowslip was used to make cordials and cakes, was candied for decorations, and made one of the most fragrant of the country wines. The leaves were also used to make tea (see page 196).

It was known in some places as palsy-wort since it was said to cure trembling of the hands, and also as herb Peter because its nodding flowers were seen as symbolic of St Peter's bunch of keys to the gates of heaven.

> I must go and seek some dew-drops here,
> And hang a pearl in every cowslip's ear.

William Shakespeare, *A Midsummer Night's Dream*

Crab-Apple (PLATE IV)

Spring and autumn

Malus sylvestris, ssp. mitis.
Rosaceae family.
Common except in Scotland.
Flowers (pink and white) April to May.
Fruits September to October.

The fruit of the wild apple tree has been eaten by man for as long as its history, and was very probably the Tree of Eden which tempted Eve and caused the Fall of Man. It is a pretty tree: both its blossoms and its fruits have a special delicate charm, and crab-apples make one of the best jellies of all the wild fruits. The addition of a few crab-apples improves an apple tart enormously.

Crab-Apple Blossom Fritters

How pretty these sound: they taste as lovely as their name. Pick the blossoms and shake them free of any insects. Dip them into fritter batter (see page 53) and deep fry at 425°F/220°C until golden brown all over. Drain on kitchen paper, dust with sieved icing sugar and serve immediately.

Crab-Apple Jelly

crab-apples
water
sugar

Cut the crab-apples into quarters and cook, with water to cover, until they are soft. Strain through a jelly-bag overnight. To every 1 pint/600 ml liquid, add ¾ lb/350 g sugar. Dissolve over a gentle heat and then boil rapidly to setting point (see page 226). Cool a little, then pot and seal.

This is the basic method for making most jellies from hedgerow fruits. Try out various combinations, for example:

1. Crab-apple and blackberry jelly (equal quantities of fruit).

2. Crab-apple and rowanberry jelly (2 parts rowan berries to 1 part crab-apples. This is delicious with game).

3. Crab-apple and hawthorn berry jelly (2 parts haws to 1 part crab-apples).

4. Crab-apple and rose-hip jelly (equal quantities of fruit).

5. The addition of a scented geranium leaf to the cooking of the crab-apples gives the jelly a wonderful flavour.

Having made your jelly, you can use the pulp left in the jelly-bag to make crab-apple cheese (see below).

Crab-Apple Cheese
❦

Mix the pulp remaining from crab-apple jelly with enough water to liquidize it in the blender, and then pass through a sieve in order to separate the pulp from the pips. To every 1 pint/600 ml pulp add $\frac{1}{2}$ lb/250 g sugar. Heat gently to boiling point, stirring to dissolve the sugar, and cook until thick. Pot and cover. You can flavour it with cinnamon at the end of the cooking if that appeals to you.

Crab-Apple Butter
❦

3 lb/1$\frac{1}{2}$ kg crab-apples
1 pint/600 ml cider
1 pint/600 ml water
2-inch/5-cm stick cinnamon
$\frac{1}{2}$ tsp cloves
sugar

Wash the crab-apples and cut them into quarters without peeling them. Cook in the cider and water until they are soft and pulpy, then put through a fine sieve. Weigh the pulp and put into a pan with the spices tied in a muslin bag and $\frac{3}{4}$ lb/350 g sugar to every 1 lb/500 g pulp. Boil, stirring frequently, until it is a thick creamy consistency. Pot in small jars and cover.

Spiced Crab-Apples
❦

1 oz/25 g each whole cloves, stick
    cinnamon and allspice berries
3 lb/1½ kg demerara sugar
2 pints/1.2 litres malt vinegar
5 lb/2½ kg crab-apples

Tie the spices in a muslin bag. Dissolve the sugar in the vinegar over a low heat and then boil with the spices for 5 minutes. Quarter and core but do not peel the crab-apples. Remove the bag, add the fruit and simmer gently until tender (about 10 minutes), making sure that they do not break. Lift from the vinegar with a slotted spoon and pack into heated jars. Re-boil the liquid until syrupy, fill the jars to the brim, and seal. These go particularly well with roast lamb or with cold pork or ham.

Glacé Crab-Apples
❦

For the glacé syrup, combine 1 lb/500 g sugar, ½ pint/300 ml water and ¼ tsp cream of tartar. Stir the sugar and water over a low heat until the sugar is dissolved, add the cream of tartar and boil rapidly to 275°F/140°C. Place the pan in cold water to stop the cooking.

Dip whole, cleaned apples in the hot syrup and then place on a baking dish and cook at 325°F/170°C or gas mark 3 for 8 to 10 minutes. Cool on a rack, store in airtight jars and serve with poultry or game.

Verjuice
❦

This is a kind of cider which is so sharp that it often used to be distilled for vinegar.

Pick ripe crab-apples and leave them in a pile until they begin to sweat. Remove the stalks and any really rotten parts, then mash the rest of the fruit and strain through a jelly-bag. Bottle the resulting liquid and leave for a month before using as a substitute for vinegar.

Lamb's Wool

And sometimes lurk I in a gossip's bowl,
In the very likeness of a roasted crab,
And when she drinks, against her lips I bob.

William Shakespeare, *A Midsummer Night's Dream*

'A universal drink for Christmas Eve, Christmas Day and Boxing Day was "lambswool" which was also drunk on other occasions such as Clemeny in November. The drink, a concoction of roasted apples in strong ale, which was spiced and sugared, was commonly given to work people by managers and small employers in South Staffordshire. It was made in large glazed earthenware vessels, known in the Black Country as a "jowl", and ladled round the company until empty, when the drinkers sang a carol.'

Jon Raven, *The Folklore of Staffordshire*
(Batsford, 1978)

Cranberry

(*Mossberry*)

Autumn

Vaccinium oxycoccos.
Ericaceae family.
Native of bogs and heaths, fairly common
in northern England, Wales and Ireland.
Height: up to 12 inches/30 cm.
Flowers (pink) from June to August.
Fruits (red) July to September.

Cranberry Sauce

½ lb/250 g cranberries
½ pint/300 ml water
sugar

Cook the cranberries in the water until they are soft. Rub through a sieve and sweeten to taste. Serve with turkey or game.

Cranberry Jelly

Make in exactly the same way as crab-apple jelly, following the instructions on page 63.

You can also make cranberry cheese (see method for bullace cheese on page 29) or use cranberries in a mixed fruit tart (see elderberry and apple tart on page 83).

Dandelion

Spring and summer

Taraxacum officinale.
Compositae family.
Very common and widespread.
Height: up to 12 inches/35 cm.
Flowers (yellow) March to September.

The dandelion may have derived its name from *dent-de-lion* (lion's tooth), a graphic description of its jagged tooth-like leaves. As an ubiquitous weed, it is well-known to children and gardeners alike, loved by the former for its wispy 'clocks', detested by the latter for its persistent growth. However, the dandelion is rich in minerals and is a versatile source of nutritious dishes: the roots can be ground and used as coffee; the flowers, picked when they are fully open in sunshine, make a lovely wine; and the leaves are delicious as a vegetable, either cooked, or raw in salads. It can be cultivated and blanched by earthing up the leaves – this process minimizes the bitter taste of the leaf – and it is sold in this form quite commonly in French markets.

Dandelion Coffee

Dig the roots in the late autumn when they are at their fattest and scrub them thoroughly. Dry them well and place in a slow oven until they are brittle. Grind them coarsely and pour boiling water over the ground roots to make the 'coffee'. The resulting drink lacks the stimulant caffeine and is considered to be a sedative.

Dandelion Roots, Oriental Style

1 cup dandelion roots
1 tbsp olive oil
water
salt and pepper
soy sauce

Scrub the roots and cut them into slices. Sauté them in the oil until they are golden and soft. Add a little water, salt and pepper. Cover and stew until tender. Sprinkle with soy sauce and serve.

Dandelion Leaves

The young raw leaves of the dandelion make a tasty addition to salads and here are a few ideas for some interesting combinations:

Sorrel and Dandelion Salad

Rub the inside of a wooden salad bowl with a cut clove of garlic. Wash the dandelion leaves and tear them into strips. Add to some lettuce leaves and dress with vinaigrette. Toss with a few sorrel leaves and some black olives. Serve with hot herb bread (see page 89).

Potato Salad with Dandelion

Cook waxy new potatoes and slice them while they are still hot. Chop a small onion, a clove of garlic and some young celery very finely. Tear some young washed dandelion leaves and toss in vinaigrette. Add to the potatoes and toss again.

Similarly, a *beetroot and dandelion salad* using young, freshly cooked beetroot is delicious. Or try an *egg and dandelion salad*: soft-boil the eggs and peel when they are cold; quarter them and place on a bed of washed, shredded dandelion leaves, dressed with a garlicky mayonnaise. Equally good is *dandelion and pasta salad*: just treat the leaves as above and add to cold pasta shapes cooked *al dente*, and dressed with oil.

Dandelion Salad au Jus

Mix dandelion leaves, washed and torn, with crisp lettuce and pour over the salad some hot gravy from a roast. Mix well and serve it with the meat.

Pissenlit au Lard

A classic French recipe for a hot and cold salad.

> a bunch of dandelion leaves
> a few lettuce leaves
> 2 shallots
> 1 clove of garlic
> salt and pepper
> olive oil
> 4 oz/100 g streaky bacon
> 2 tbsps vinegar

Mix washed, torn dandelion leaves with the lettuce, chopped shallots, crushed garlic and seasonings. Dress with the oil and toss well.

Cut the bacon into dice and fry in a hot ungreased pan until all the fat runs and the bacon is crisp.

Pour the vinegar into the pan, cook until it is well reduced and pour over the salad with the bacon. Toss quickly and serve immediately.

Dandelion Sandwich

Butter a thin slice of white bread and sprinkle with a dash of Worcestershire sauce. Place a good layer of washed, finely chopped dandelion leaves on the bread and cover with a thin slice of buttered brown bread.

Dandelion Leaves as a Cooked Vegetable

Cook young, washed leaves in boiling water for a few minutes until tender. Drain, and press them dry with a wooden spoon. Toss with a generous knob of butter and serve. Garnish with fried breadcrumbs.

Alternatively, pour hot gravy or seasoned cream over the cooked leaves and serve immediately; or add to a little béchamel sauce (see page 224).

Stewed Dandelion Leaves

1 pint/600 ml dandelion leaves, well
 pressed down
1 oz/25 g butter
1 tsp flour
2–3 tbsps cream or stock

Wash the leaves and cook in boiling salted water for a few minutes until they are tender. Melt the butter and add the flour. Stir in the hot cream or stock gradually until the sauce thickens, then add the dandelion leaves and stir until the mixture is thoroughly hot. Serve with triangles of fried bread.

Dandelion leaves can also be used in soups; for example, they can be added to nettle soup (see page 150), to nettle and watercress soup, to sorrel and lettuce soup or to lettuce soup.

Dandelion Tea

Infuse a few leaves – fresh or dried – in boiling water for 3 or 4 minutes. Strain and drink sweetened with honey. (See Teas, page 196.)

Dandelion Flowers

Dandelion Flower Wine

For 1 gallon/4 litres wine:

3 quarts/3.5 litres dandelion heads,
 with all the stalks removed, picked in
 sunshine when the flowers are fully
 out
8 oz/250 g sultanas
3 lb/1½ kg sugar
1 orange
1 lemon
1 quart/1 litre water
¾ oz/20 g baker's yeast

Make the wine following the instructions for flower wines on page 222.

Deadnettle

Summer

Labiatae family.

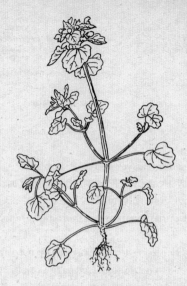

(a) Red Deadnettle (PLATE II)
Lamium purpureum.

(b) White Deadnettle (PLATE II)
Lamium album.

*A widespread native perennial, found on
hedgebanks and verges, except in northern
Scotland and Northern Ireland.
Height: up to 20 inches/50 cm.
Flowers from March to November.*

The flowers of the deadnettle can be candied (see method on page 94).
Another use for them is mentioned in Gerard's *Herball*: 'As also the
distilled water of them, which is used to make the heart merry, to make a
good colour in the face, and to refresh the vitall spirits.' The young leaves
and shoots can be cooked like spinach and are delicious tossed in butter.

Dewberry

Autumn

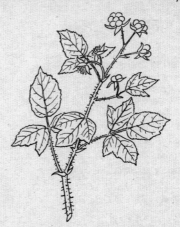

Rubus caesius.
Rosaceae family.
Common in the south and east; native.
Trailing stems reach up to 10 feet/3 m.
Fruits August to October with bluish
berries.

The dewberry or stone bramble looks very like the blackberry bramble but the beautiful lavender-blue fruits have fewer segments. Unfortunately, the berries are seldom large or plentiful: when they are, however, the flavour is marvellous and they can be used in the same ways as blackberries.

Dock

Spring and summer

Polygonaceae family

(a) Broad-Leaved Dock (PLATE II)
Rumex obtusifolius.
Native perennial, very common.
Height: up to 3 feet/1 m.
Flowers May to October.

(b) Curled Dock
Rumex crispus

(c) Sharp Pointed Dock
Rumex acetus.
Common and widespread on verges and in
the hedgerows.
Height: up to 3 feet/1 m.

Broad-leaved dock (left)
Curled dock (right)

Dock is related to sorrel and, when the leaves are young, they have a similar refreshing taste. They can be gathered throughout the growing season before the plant flowers and runs to seed. When farmers cut back their verges, the vigorous dock grows again within a couple of weeks. Dock leaves were used in the old days to wrap the butter to take to market. When blanched, their taste is reminiscent of vine leaves.

Stuffed Dock Leaves

12–18 young dock leaves
boiling water
olive oil

Wash the leaves and blanch them by placing them in a dish and covering them with boiling water. Leave for a few minutes and then drain. Repeat the process if they are not quite soft enough, but the leaves are fragile and you need to be careful that they do not disintegrate. Dry them and brush both sides with olive oil.

For the stuffing:
1 small onion
$\frac{1}{2}$ oz/15 g butter
2 oz/50 g walnuts
2 tsps grated horseradish
2 tbsps double cream
salt and pepper
2 oz/50 g rice, cooked
1 egg yolk, beaten

Chop the onion finely and cook gently in the melted butter until it is very soft. Chop the walnuts very finely and mix with the horseradish. Add to the onion and gradually stir in the cream. When it is a thick moist consistency, season to taste, add to the cooked rice and bind with the egg yolk.

Place a spoonful of stuffing in the centre of each leaf, roll it up and wrap into a little parcel. Brush with olive oil and serve cold as an appetizer.

For hot stuffed dock leaves, use the chestnut stuffing on page 35, or make a conventional mincemeat and herb stuffing.

Dock Leaves with Mushrooms

Wash and blanch young dock leaves as above, drain them, dry them and brush both sides with olive oil.

Place a cleaned mushroom in the centre of each leaf, season with salt, pepper and crushed garlic. Wrap the leaves around the mushrooms to make little parcels, and put in a greased baking dish. Cover with more blanched dock leaves brushed with olive oil. Cook covered with foil for $\frac{1}{2}$ hour at 350°F/180°C or gas mark 4. Serve hot as an hors d'œuvre or cold with pre-dinner drinks.

Douglas Fir

Spring

Pseudotsuga menziesii.
Pinaceae family.
Height: up to 160 feet/50 m.

The tips of the young shoots of Douglas fir picked in the spring give a subtle, woody flavour to food with which they are cooked. They can also be used in marinades for barbecued meat and poultry.

Try placing 6 or 8 fir tips on a roast of spring lamb while it is cooking.

Or make stock in the normal way but infuse the fir tips until they have imparted their flavour, then use the stock for soups and casseroles.

Elder

Spring, summer
and autumn

Sambucus nigra.
Caprifoliaceae family.
Native, common and widespread.
Height: up to 22 feet/7 m.
Flowers (white) May and June.
Fruits (dark red) August to November.

Elderflower

Elder has the reputation of being an unlucky tree – maybe because there is a tradition that it was the wood used to make Christ's cross, and Judas reputedly hung himself from an elder tree. It was believed that burning elder in your hearth allows bad spirits into your home, and to this day woodmen still dislike felling elders. Conversely however they were often planted near homes as a protection against evil.

Elder is a very hard wood and there is a Sussex saying:

> An eldern stake and blackthorn ether
> Will make a hedge last for ever.

Be that as it may, the elder produces edible buds, flowers and berries which can provide a wide repertoire of interesting and delicious tastes. The leaves can also be used to make tea (see page 196).

Pickled Elderbuds

These have a taste reminiscent of bamboo shoots and were a popular pickle in the eighteenth century.

Strip the buds off their stalks and put into a brine made with 6 oz/175 g salt to 1 quart/1 litre water, for a week. Drain. Put into a preserving pan, cover with spiced vinegar (see page 28) and heat through gently. Cool and re-heat twice. Cool, put the buds into jars and cover with the vinegar. Seal and store.

Elderflowers (Summer)

The beautifully-scented creamy sprays of elder blossoms impart a delicious and delicate muscatel flavour to whatever they are cooked with, and are well-known for their special affinity with gooseberries. Vinegar can be flavoured with elderflowers (see page 198). The flowers can also be used to make original summer drinks which are enjoyed as much by children as by adults.

Elderflower Cordial

This recipe was given to me by a neighbour, and for several years now the results have been in great demand. So here it is – and so easy too:

> 20 heads of elderflowers
> $3\frac{1}{2}$ lb/1.75 kg sugar
> 3 pints/1.8 litres boiled water, cold
> 2 oz/50 g tartaric acid
> 2 sliced lemons

Put all the ingredients into a large pan and stir periodically for 24 hours. Strain and bottle.

Dilute to taste with water or mineral water. It is ready to drink immediately but it will keep for several months and has an elusive taste – a cross between lychees and muscat grapes.

Elderflower Fizz

> 1 gallon/4 litres water
> $1\frac{1}{2}$ lb/750 g sugar
> 2 large heads of elderflowers
> 1 lemon and 1 orange
> 2 tbsps white wine vinegar

Boil the water and pour it over the sugar. When it is cold, add the elderflowers, the sliced lemon and orange, and the vinegar. Cover with a thick cloth and leave for 24 hours.

Squeeze the flowers and strain through a fine sieve. Store in large containers. The elderflower fizz is ready after a fortnight and is best drunk cold.

Elderflower Wine
❦

For 1 gallon/4 litres wine:
1 pint/600 ml elderflower heads, well
   pressed down
2 lemons
2½ lb/1¼ kg sugar
½ oz/15 g baker's yeast
8 oz/250 g sultanas
1 quart/1 litre water

Make the wine following instructions for flower wines on page 222.

Elderflower Fritters
❦

2 heads of elderflowers per person
fritter batter (see page 53)
sugar
cinnamon or chopped sweet cicely (see
   page 192)

Shake the flowers free of insects and make sure that they are dry. Strip the flowers off their stalks into the batter and mix in well. Deep fry spoonfuls of the mixture at 425°F/220°C, until golden brown on both sides. Drain on kitchen paper and sprinkle with sugar mixed with either a little cinnamon or with chopped sweet cicely. Serve hot with ice cream or yoghurt.

Elderflower Pancakes
❦

Add flowerets to pancake batter (see page 225) in the same way as for the fritters (see above), cook the pancakes in the usual way and serve with lemon quarters and sugar.

Elderflower Islands

2 elderflower heads
1 pint/600 ml milk
2 eggs, separated
2 oz/50 g sugar
1½ tbsps cornflour
1½ oz/40 g caster sugar
cinnamon

Shake the flowers clean and strip them from their stalks. Infuse in the simmering milk for 10 minutes.

Beat the egg yolks with the 2 oz/50 g sugar until thick and pale yellow, and then whisk in the sieved cornflour. Add the hot, strained milk gradually, stirring all the time. Put over a low heat and stir until thick. Put into glasses or bowls.

Beat the egg whites with the 1½ oz/40 g caster sugar until very stiff, and float tablespoons of the mixture on top of the custard. Chill. Sprinkle with caster sugar and cinnamon and serve. For 4.

Elderflower Sorbet

grated rind and juice of 3 lemons
6 oz/175 g sugar
1 pint/600 ml water
3 elderflower heads
1 egg white

Combine the lemon rinds, sugar, water and elderflowers and dissolve the sugar over a low heat. Bring to the boil and cook rapidly for 6 to 10 minutes. Cool. Add the lemon juice, strain and freeze.

After about an hour, when the sorbet is turning mushy, beat it up with a whisk and then fold in the stiffly beaten egg white. Re-freeze, stir again after another hour and leave to set. Serve garnished with mint sprigs. For 6.

Gooseberry and Elderflower Sorbet

Make ¾ pint/450 ml gooseberry and elderflower compote (see below) and freeze it. Make the sorbet as above.

Gooseberry and Elderflower Compote

> 4 oz/100 g sugar
> ½ pint/300 ml water
> 1 lb/500 g gooseberries
> 2 elderflower heads, tied in a muslin
>   bag

Make a syrup by dissolving the sugar in the water and boiling it for 5 minutes. Put the gooseberries in the syrup with the elderflowers and cook very gently for 10 minutes. Remove the flowers and cool the gooseberries. Serve chilled in three or four glass bowls. You can also make a delicious rhubarb and elderflower compote in just the same way.

Gooseberry and Elderflower Jam

> 3 lb/1½ kg gooseberries
> 2 pints/1.2 litres water
> 6 large elderflower heads, tied in a
>   muslin bag
> 4 lb/2 kg sugar

Simmer the gooseberries in the water with the bag of flowers for ½ hour. Remove the flowers, add the sugar and stir until dissolved. Boil to setting point, pot and cover.

Gooseberry and Elderflower Jelly

Follow the instructions for crab-apple jelly on page 63, using gooseberries to make the jelly. When boiling to setting point, dip some elderflower heads tied in a muslin bag (2 heads to every 4 lb or 2 kg fruit) into the mixture until it is well flavoured but not overpoweringly so. Pot and seal.

Elderberries (Autumn)

John Evelyn said of the elderberry that it was 'a catholicon against all infirmities whatever'. Be that as it may, this fruit is generally underestimated and greatly under-used. The elderberry has a wonderful flavour which is not unlike blackcurrant, and can be made up into many delicious dishes, sauces and preserves.

Elderberry

Elderberry Crumble

2 lb/1 kg elderberries
4 oz/100 g sugar

For the crumble:
8 oz/250 g flour
a pinch of salt
4 oz/100 g butter
5 oz/150 g sugar (soft brown and white
    mixed)
a pinch of soda bicarbonate
cinnamon

Half-fill a baking dish with ripe elderberries, stripped from their stalks. Sprinkle with the 4 oz/100 g sugar and shake until the berries are well coated.

Sift the flour with the salt and rub the butter into it. Add the 5 oz/150 g sugar, soda bicarbonate and cinnamon. Mix well. Cover the elderberries with the crumble and cook at 375°F/190°C or gas mark 5 for 35 minutes. Serve with cream. For 4.

Alternatively, you can use an equal quantity of apples and elderberries.

Elderberry and Apple Tart

8 oz/250 g sweet crust pastry
1 lb/500 g apples
½ lb/250 g elderberries
4 oz/100 g sugar

Line a greased 8-inch/20-cm flan dish with half the pastry, rolled out thinly. Peel, core and slice the apples and put into the pastry shell. Put the elderberries on top and sprinkle with the sugar. Cover with the remaining pastry and press the edges together with a fork. Brush with milk and bake at 350°F/180°C or gas mark 4 for 25 to 30 minutes. Serve hot or cold with ice cream. For 4.

Elderberry Sorbet

1 lb/500 g elderberries
juice of ½ a lemon
4 oz/100 g sugar
½ pint/300 ml water
2 egg whites

Wash the elderberries and liquidize them with a little sugar. Sieve them, to separate the pulp from the pips. Add the lemon juice. Make the sorbet as for cloudberry sorbet on page 46. Serves 4.

Elderberry Ice Cream

8 oz/250 g elderberries
2½ oz/60 g caster sugar
a small carton of double cream
1½ oz/40 g icing sugar
2 egg whites

Wash the berries and liquidize with the sugar. Sieve, to separate the pulp from the pips. Whip the cream with the sifted icing sugar until it is thick. Fold into the purée. Whisk the egg whites until stiff and fold into the mixture. Cover and freeze.

Elderberry Curd

❄

1 lb/500 g elderberries
4 oz/100 g butter
12 oz/300 g sugar
4 eggs

Wash the berries and cook in a little water until they are soft. Sieve, to separate the pulp from the pips, and put the purée in a bowl with the butter and the sugar. Place over simmering water until the sugar has dissolved, stirring well. Beat the eggs, add to the fruit purée and stir over the hot water until the mixture thickens. Pot, cover and store in a cool place.

This makes a delicious filling for dessert pancakes, sprinkled with lemon juice and sugar.

Elderberry Catsup or Ketchup (Pontack Sauce)

❄

¾ pint/450 ml vinegar
1 lb/500 g ripe elderberries
4 shallots
½ tsp salt
1 slice of root ginger
1 blade of mace
40 peppercorns
12 cloves

Boil the vinegar and pour over the elderberries in a glazed earthenware dish. Stand, covered, in a cool oven (225°F/110°C or gas mark ¼) overnight. Strain. Boil the liquid for 10 minutes with the sliced shallots, salt and spices. When it is cold, bottle it and store for at least 1 year – it is said to be at its best after 7 years!

This sauce, strained before being used, goes beautifully with fish, and it is also very good with liver dishes.

A vinegar flavoured with elderberries can also be made (see page 198).

Spiced Elderberry Jelly

To serve with cold meats or poultry.

> 1 lb/500 g apples
> ¾ pint/450 ml water
> 4 lb/2 kg elderberries
> loaf sugar
> 4 cloves
> a 3-inch/8-cm stick of cinnamon

Core but do not peel the apples. Chop and cook to a pulp in the water. Add the elderberries, washed and stripped from their stalks, and cook for 30 minutes. Strain through a jelly-bag overnight, measure the juice and to every 1 pint/600 ml add 8 oz/250 g loaf sugar. Put in a pan with the spices tied in a muslin bag and heat gently until the sugar has dissolved. Boil to setting point, remove the spices, pot and seal.

To make *Elderberry Jelly*, follow the recipe for crab-apple jelly on page 63.

To make mixed jellies, use equal quantities of elderberries to other fruits and make by the same method.

1. Elderberry and apple jelly.
2. Elderberry and blackberry jelly.
3. Elderberry and crab-apple jelly.
4. Elderberry, damson, apple and blackberry jelly.
5. Elderberry and ginger jelly (cook a piece of bruised root ginger with every 1 lb/500 g fruit).

Elderberry and Blackberry Jam

> 2 lb/1 kg elderberries
> 2 lb/1 kg blackberries
> 2 lb/1 kg sugar
> juice of ½ a lemon

Wash the elderberries and strip them from their stalks. Mix with the blackberries and simmer in a little water until they are soft (20 to 25 minutes). Sieve, to separate the pulp from the pips. Add the sugar and the lemon juice to the pulp, dissolve over a low heat, then bring to the boil and cook until setting point is reached. Pot and cover.

It is important to strain out all the pips as otherwise the texture of the jam is unappetizing. The addition of lemon juice to elderberry lightens its dense flavour and is, to my taste, an improvement.

Here are some suggestions for variations on this jam:

1. Elderberry and plum jam.
2. Elderberry and apple jam.
3. Elderberry, blackberry, sloe, crab-apple and cobs – the ultimate in hedgerow jam! (The chopped nuts are added towards the end of the cooking process, after the sieving.)

Elderberry Wine

Here is Dorothy Wise's recipe from *Home Made Country Wines* (Hamlyn, 1971).

> '4–5 lb of elderberries
> 1 gallon of water
> 3½ lb sugar
> 1 lemon
> ½ oz root ginger (if liked)
> 6 cloves (if liked)
> ¾ oz baker's yeast, or a wine yeast (I
> used a Burgundy yeast)

'*Method:* Strip the berries from the stalks with a fork. Put into a large bowl. Pour over the water boiling, stir and mash with a wooden spoon. Leave for 3 days, stirring daily. Strain into a pan with the thinly peeled rind of the lemon, and the spices. Bruise the ginger well. Bring to the boil, and simmer for 10 minutes. Allow to cool, then strain over the sugar and stir well. Add the lemon juice, and lastly when the liquid is lukewarm, add the yeast. Baker's yeast can be creamed with a little of the warm liquid first. A wine yeast should be activated 2 days before needed.'

Elm (English)

Spring

Ulmus procera.
Ulmaceae family.
A native hardwood which resists wetting
and splitting.
Height: up to 100 feet/30 m.
Flowers (red-brown) in February and
March.
Fruits (round, green, winged seeds) in
May.
Leaves: dark green and rough with
downy central vein.

> The moan of doves in immemorial elms,
> And murmuring of innumerable bees.
>
> Alfred, Lord Tennyson, 'The Princess'

The elm remains an important part of our natural and folkloric heritage. It was once called 'elven' as it was closely associated with elves. Now so sadly ravaged by Dutch elm disease, it seems scarcely graceful to mention that the young raw leaves of this magnificent tree can be eaten in green salads: the death of so many elms would make eating any part of its growth seem criminal.

Fat Hen (PLATE II)

(*White Goosefoot*)

Summer

Chenopodium album.
Chenopodiaceae family.
Native annual of waste places and arable
land (particularly beet fields). Common
throughout Britain.
Height: up to 3 feet/1 m.
Leaves dusty silvery green; flowers
(mealy green spikes) July to October.

Fat hen has been for me the most enlightening discovery of all my forays into the hedgerows: I had never heard of it before, even less did I know that it had been a staple vegetable throughout history – from Neolithic times down to the last century, when it was superseded by cultivated varieties of spinach, its relative. I tried it tentatively and was astonished at how similar in texture it was to broccoli, and how distinguished its own flavour. I had difficulty in restraining not only myself but also my five-year-old daughter from over-indulging!

Fat hen used also to be known as 'all-good', for it is a rich source of protein, has prodigious quantities of vitamins B_1 and B_2, and more iron and calcium than spinach. It suffers from having many common names that lend themselves to ridicule – such as 'dirty dick', 'mutton tops', 'pig-weed' and 'lambs' quarters' – but don't let that deter you: it is a sensational vegetable.

It is such an abundant and vigorous weed that once you find an area where it grows you may very possibly be able to pick great armfuls to carry home triumphant to your kitchen. When blanched, it freezes extremely well, as it does also when made up into soup.

To Cook Fat Hen

Strip off the thin young leaf stems, including the mealy spikes but avoiding the thicker stalks which will be tough and woody. Wash them and cook in their own water with some salt, as you would for spinach. Simmer for 10 to 12 minutes, drain, chop and remove any stalks that have remained woody.

Fat Hen Soup

1 lb/500 g fat hen, cooked
6 oz/175 g rice, cooked
1½ pints/1 litre stock
salt and pepper
a little cream

Liquidize the fat hen and rice with the stock until thoroughly blended. Thin out with extra stock if necessary. Season and finish with cream. Heat through and serve with hot herb bread (see below). For 4.

Herb Bread

Slice a loaf of French bread down the middle and butter it thickly. Chop finely a mixture or selection of the following herbs: chamomile, dandelion, yarrow, cow parsley, rocket, thyme, bittercress, borage, chives, garlic mustard, nasturtium leaves, tansy.

Press them into the butter and put the two halves of the loaf back together again. Wrap securely in foil and bake at 400°F/200°C or gas mark 6 for 15 minutes. Slice crosswise and serve hot.

Fat Hen and Ham Croûtes

1½ lb/750 g fat hen, cooked
butter
salt, pepper and nutmeg
4 slices of bread
clarified butter
4 slices of good ham
¾ pint/450 ml *sauce à la crème* (see page 224)

Toss the hot, drained fat hen in butter with salt, pepper and a little nutmeg.

Fry the bread in clarified butter (see page 225) until golden, then turn the slices of ham in the butter to heat through. Place on the fried bread in a baking dish, put a quarter of the fat hen on top of each slice of ham, cover with a spoonful or two of the sauce, heat through rapidly in a very hot oven and serve immediately. For 4.

Fat Hen Croquettes

1 lb/500 g fat hen, cooked
½ lb/250 g mashed potatoes
1 egg, beaten
breadcrumbs
parsley

Chop the fat hen and mix well with the potato. Chill. Shape into croquettes, brush with the beaten egg and roll in breadcrumbs. Fry in hot fat until golden brown all over and serve with sprigs of fried parsley on top. For 4.

Fat Hen Daisy

1 lb/500 g mushrooms
butter
¾ pint/450 ml béchamel sauce (see page 224)
cream
salt and pepper
2 lb/1 kg fat hen, cooked
1 oz/25 g parmesan cheese, grated

Chop the mushrooms finely and cook in butter until they are soft. Mix with half the béchamel and add a little cream. Season to taste.

Season the fat hen and make layers in a buttered fireproof dish with the mushroom mixture and the fat hen, ending with the fat hen. Add the Parmesan to the remaining béchamel with a little cream and freshly ground black pepper, and pour over the top. Dot with butter and bake at 350°F/180°C or gas mark 4 for 30 minutes. Serves 4.

Fat Hen and Anchovy Pie

1½ lb/750 g fat hen, cooked
salt and pepper
2 oz/50 g grated Parmesan cheese
1 lb/500 g potatoes
2 tbsps mashed anchovies
2 oz/50 g softened butter
1 oz/25 g grated Cheddar cheese, mixed
    with 1 oz/25 g breadcrumbs

Drain and chop the fat hen, season and mix with the Parmesan. Peel the potatoes, slice them about ¼ inch/½ cm thick and boil them for 5 minutes in salted water. Butter a baking dish, place half the potatoes over the bottom and season them. Cover with the fat hen, then make another layer of potatoes. Add the anchovies to the softened butter and spread over the potatoes. Finish with a layer of the fat hen. Sprinkle with the Cheddar cheese and breadcrumb mixture, dot with butter and cook at 375°F/190°C or gas mark 5 for 25 minutes. Serves 4.

Fat Hen au Gratin with Eggs

1½ lb/750 g fat hen, cooked
butter
salt and pepper
4 soft-boiled eggs
1 pint/600 ml *sauce à la crème* (see page
    224
2 oz/50 g fried breadcrumbs

Drain and chop the fat hen, toss in butter and season to taste. Cover the bottom of a fireproof dish with the fat hen, then place the halved eggs on top. Pour over them the sauce, dot with butter and cook at 400°F/200°C or gas mark 6 for 20 minutes or until the top is golden. Sprinkle with the fried breadcrumbs. Serves 4.

Fat Hen Soufflé

> grated Parmesan cheese
> 2 shallots
> a pat of butter for cooking the shallots
> 6 oz/175 g fat hen, cooked
> salt, pepper, cayenne and nutmeg
> 2 oz/50 g butter
> 1½ oz/40 g flour
> ½ pint/300 ml hot milk
> 4 eggs, separated

Butter a soufflé dish and sprinkle with cheese, knocking out any excess that does not stick to the sides.

Cook the chopped shallots in butter very gently until they are soft, then add the cooked fat hen and stir over a moderate heat. Season.

In another pan, melt the 2 oz/50 g butter, add the flour and stir in the hot milk until the mixture thickens. Simmer gently for a few minutes and season to taste.

Off the heat, beat the egg yolks into the sauce base one by one and then add the vegetable mixture. Beat the whites with a pinch of salt until they are stiff. Fold into the base mixture half at a time and turn into the soufflé dish. Sprinkle with grated Parmesan and put into the oven, pre-heated to 400°F/200°C or gas mark 6. Turn the heat down to 375°F/190°C or gas mark 5 and cook for 25 to 30 minutes. Serves 4.

Here are some more suggestions for using fat hen:

1. Simply serve it as you would spinach, tossed in butter or in *beurre noir* (see page 225).

2. Moisten with gravy or cream and serve with roast meats.

3. Prepare a bed of fat hen on a baking dish and keep hot. Fry some eggs in very hot fat until crisp and place on top. Add a dash of vinegar and a finely chopped shallot to the fat in the pan and let it sizzle. Pour over the eggs and serve immediately.

4. Line ramekins with cooked fat hen, put peeled prawns in the middle, cover with cream and heat through for an hors d'œuvre.

5. Use as a filling for an omelette, or as a base for poached eggs, or in *œufs florentines*.

6. Cover a layer of fat hen with crisply fried rashers of bacon and serve with triangles of fresh bread.

7. Cold cooked fat hen is delicious in sandwiches or on bread and butter. It also makes a good salad, tossed in vinaigrette and garnished with hard-boiled eggs.

8. Creamed fat hen makes a delicious filling for pancakes, pastry triangles and savoury profiteroles (see pages 55–6).

Flowers

Left to right
Top row: *Carnation, Borage, Forget-me-not,
Apple blossom*
Middle row: *Marigold, Rose, Narcissus*
Bottom row: *Violet, Primrose, Daisy*

Bring the rathe primrose that forsaken dies,
The tufted crow-toe and pale jasmine,
The white pink, and pansy freaked with jet,
The glowing violet, the musk rose and the well-attired woodbine;
With cowslips wan that hang the pensive head,
And every flower that sad embroidery wears.

John Milton, 'Lycidas'

Many wild flowers can be crystallized or candied and used to decorate cakes, puddings and ices. Primroses, cowslips, borage flowers, rose petals, mint, violets, red deadnettle, crab-apple blossom, daisies, forget-me-nots, narcissi, apple blossom, almond blossom, jasmine, carnations and rose-buds can all be preserved in this way.

Roses, marigolds and nasturtiums are particularly versatile in cookery and have sections of their own.

To Candy Flowers (1)

3 tsps gum arabic
3 tbsps orange flower water

Put the crystals in a small bottle or jar and cover with the orange flower water. Leave to dissolve for 3 days, shaking frequently.

Pick the flowers and make sure that they are free from dust or moisture. Using a small paintbrush, cover all the surfaces of the flowers with the solution, separating the petals carefully. Try holding the flower with tweezers to ensure that every part of its area is coated.

Sprinkle with caster sugar and shake off any excess. Dry on paper in a warm cupboard, then store in airtight jars.

To Candy Flowers (2)

1 cup sugar
$\frac{1}{2}$ cup water

Cook the sugar and the water to 240°F/115°C. Dip the flowers into the syrup, coat with caster sugar and dry on a rack. Store in airtight containers.

To Crystallize Petals and Leaves

Beat an egg white until stiff. Dip the freshly picked, cleaned and dry leaf or petal into the egg white, holding it with tweezers to make sure that the entire surface is covered. Sprinkle both sides with caster sugar and dry on a rack in a slow oven (250°F/130°C or gas mark $\frac{1}{2}$) for several hours. Store in airtight jars.

Flower Conserve

4 lb/2 kg cooking apples
2 pints/1.2 litres water
8 oz/250 g mixed flower petals (see
  above)
sugar

Cut the apples into pieces without peeling or coring them. Cook with the water and the petals until the fruit is soft. Strain through a jelly-bag overnight. To each 1 pint/600 ml juice add $\frac{3}{4}$ lb/350 g sugar. Dissolve over a low heat, bring to the boil and cook rapidly to setting point. Pot and seal.

Flower Ice Cream

2 eggs, separated
3 oz/75 g granulated sugar
½ pint/300 ml double cream
¼ tsp orange flower water
½ cupful mixed flower petals

Beat the egg yolks with the sugar until thick and pale yellow. Heat half of the cream and beat it in, then put into a bowl over hot water and stir until thick. Add the orange flower water and the petals and stir. Let it stand for ½ hour, then strain and cool.

Whip the rest of the cream and fold it into the mixture. Beat the egg whites until stiff, fold into the cream and put in a container. Cover and freeze.

Candied Flower Cream

½ lb/250 g each cottage cheese and
  cream cheese
6 oz/175 g caster sugar
1 large carton double cream
1 teacup candied petals (see above)
sherry or a liqueur

Mash the cottage cheese with the cream cheese and caster sugar in a bowl with a fork until smooth. Beat the cream, add to the cheese mixture and chill.

Put the petals into a bowl and sprinkle with the sherry or liqueur. Leave to stand overnight.

Fold the petals into the cream, including the juices. Mix well and pile into glasses. Garnish each glass with a candied flower and serve with almond biscuits.

Carnation Petal Cream

For my part, as a thing to keep and not to sell; as a thing, the possession of which is to give me pleasure, I hesitate not a moment to prefer the plant of a fine carnation, to a gold watch set with diamonds.

William Cobbett, *The American Gardener*

Fold the petals, a few at a time, into sweetened cream. Stand in a cool place until ready for use. Remove the petals and whip the cream. It goes beautifully with pears poached in vanilla syrup, or with fresh strawberries or blackberries.

This can also be made using sweet william petals or geranium leaves.

Carnation Liqueur

½ lb/250 g carnation petals
2 pints/1 litre 39° alcohol
1 clove
½-inch/1-cm stick cinnamon
1 lb/500 g sugar
1 pint/600 ml water

Steep the petals in the alcohol with the spices. Filter after 1 month.

Make a syrup with the sugar and water and add to the alcohol. Strain and bottle.

Garlic Mustard (PLATE III)

(Jack-by-the-Hedge)

Spring and summer

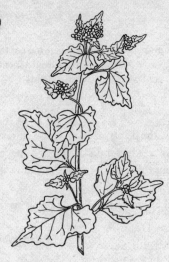

Alliaria petiolata.
Cruciferae family.
Native biennial, common in hedgerows
and on verges in England.
Height: up to 3 feet/1 m.
Flowers (cream and white) April to
June.

The jagged leaves of this widespread plant smell of garlic when they are crushed, and in the old days were commonly used in salads or for flavouring stews.

Try adding young chopped leaves to a cheese sandwich, eating them on fresh buttered bread or mixing them with potted meats. Culpeper recommends their use in salads (always pick the young leaves since, in most cases, the older leaves of hedgerow plants tend to become bitter or even to change their flavour entirely). Garlic mustard can be used to flavour butter to serve with fish, or made into the following sauce:

Garlic Mustard Sauce

To serve with lamb.

> 1 handful each garlic mustard leaves
>   and hawthorn buds
> a sprig of mint
> vinegar
> sugar

Chop all the leaves finely and mix with the buds and the vinegar. Add sugar to taste and serve instead of mint sauce.

Fried Herrings with Garlic Mustard

8 oz/250 g streaky bacon
4 herrings
flour
salt and pepper
2 tbsps olive oil
1 large handful garlic mustard leaves

Fry the bacon until it is crisp. Dip the herrings into well-seasoned flour and fry in butter until golden brown and cooked through. Keep hot with the bacon crumbled over the top. In a separate pan heat the oil until it is smoking and then fry the garlic mustard leaves very rapidly until they are crisp. Drain on a kitchen towel and sprinkle over the herrings. Serve with mashed potatoes and a green salad. Serves 4.

Golden Saxifrage

Spring and early summer

Chrysosplenium oppositifolium.
Saxifragaceae family.
Native perennial, fairly common, found
on stream banks and in wet places.
Height: up to 4 inches/10 cm.
Flowers (yellow-green) April to July.

Golden saxifrage may be eaten as a vegetable. Cook the young leaves and shoots in boiling salted water for 10 to 15 minutes and serve with butter.

Good King Henry

(*Goosefoot*)

Summer

Chenopodium bonus-henricus.
Chenopodiaceae family.
Fairly common in England and Wales.
Height: up to 20 inches/50 cm.
Flowers (reddish mealy spikes) May to
July.

A close relative of fat hen, the leaves of this plant can be used in all the same ways (see pages 88–93). Good king henry was cultivated quite commonly in medieval and Tudor times. The young leaves are extremely good in salads, and the young shoots make a tasty cooked vegetable when dipped in melted butter and eaten like asparagus; the older leaves should be cooked just like spinach and served tossed in butter.

King Henry's Salad

Dice the flesh of a ripe avocado pear. Cook some strips of streaky bacon until they are crisp. Wash and chop some young leaves of good king henry and toss them all together in a garlicky vinaigrette.

Goosegrass

(*Cleavers, Sticky Willie*)

Spring and summer

Galium aparine.
Rubiaceae family.
Native annual, very common.
Flowers (white) May to August.

This rampant plant is actually edible although possibly more suited to the diet of the goose than to that of the human being. It is said that the young leaves, picked before the seeds appear in May, can be picked and eaten like spinach, but I have not been tempted. There is an alarming Elizabethan recipe for a 'pottage' of goosegrass and oatmeal, which was eaten to cause 'lankenesse': slimming gone mad. I think it was that that deterred me.

Ground Elder (PLATE III)

(*Bishop's Weed, Goutweed*)

Summer

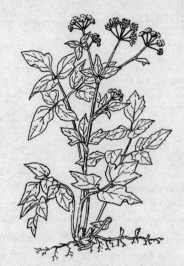

Aegopodium podagraria.
Umbelliferae family.
Perennial, very common.
Height: up to 3 feet/90 cm.
Flowers (white) May to July.

Who would have believed that this ubiquitous weed, well-known to the despairing gardener, was edible, let alone worth the trouble of picking and cooking? Well, it is, and was in fact originally introduced by the Romans as a culinary plant and cultivated throughout the Middle Ages. It has a delicate and distinctive taste and well deserves a place in the repertoire of the vegetable cook. So when it rampages over your garden, don't despair, eat it.

It is called ground elder because its leaves look so similar to those of the common elder, but they are not related. Ground elder was dedicated to St Gerard who was traditionally invoked to cure gout, and the Romans are known to have used it to this end.

To Cook Ground Elder

Pick the young leaf stems. Wash and cook them in a little boiling, salted water for about 10 minutes. Drain well and toss with butter.

Alternatively, add them to a little béchamel sauce (see page 224), or to well-seasoned cream, and serve as a side vegetable.

Guelder Rose (PLATE III)

Autumn

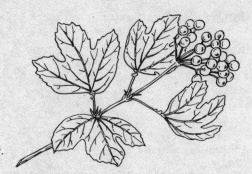

Viburnum opulus.
Caprifoliaceae family.
Native and common.
Height: up to 18 feet/5 m.
Fruits August to November.

This lovely shrub with its beautiful clusters of scarlet berries is often found near water and in damp woodland and hedgerows. The waxy fruits are not edible raw but can be cooked to make a jam or jelly which makes a good substitute for one made of cranberries. The leaves turn a brilliant red in autumn.

Guelder Rose Jelly

Follow the instructions for crab-apple jelly on page 63; and serve with roast turkey or game.

Hawthorn (PLATE IV)

(*May*)

Spring and autumn

Crataegus monogyna.
Rosaceae family.
Native and very common.
Height: up to 25 feet/8 m.
Flowers (white) May and June.
Berries (red) August to November.

Hawthorn flower

> Gives not the hawthorn bush a sweeter shade
> To shepherds, looking on their silly sheep,
> Than doth a rich embroidered canopy
> To kings that fear their subjects' treachery?
>
> William Shakespeare, *Henry IV, Part 1*

In folklore the budding of the may tree signifies the end of winter and heralds the oncoming spring: hence the origin of May Day. It used to fall on 12 May until the calendar changes of 1752, so now the hawthorn is rarely in flower by the national holiday on 1 May. Traditionally, young girls bathed in hawthorn dew on May Morning in the hope of becoming more beautiful:

> The fair maid who the first of May
> Goes to the field at the break of day,
> And washes in dew from the hawthorn tree,
> Will ever after handsome be.

The hawthorn was said to have healing powers and also to offer protection against lightning:

Beware of an oak,
It draws the stroke,
Avoid the ash,
It courts the flash,
Creep under the thorn,
It will save you from harm.

But above all hawthorn is a symbol of re-birth and life – some legends say that Christ wore a crown of hawthorn. It is also traditionally the tree of lovers, the smell of may blossom being, so they say, aphrodisiac. Perhaps for that reason there is an old wives' tale that says it is unlucky to cut down a hawthorn tree or to bring cut branches into the house – indeed to bring may flowers indoors was thought to forebode a death.

Hawthorn is extremely hardy and long-lived and is the most commonly planted hedge shrub in Britain: 'haw' is from an Old English word for hedge. Young hawthorn leaves are well-known to children as 'bread and cheese', the berries are edible and the blossom has its uses too.

May Drink

1 pint/600 ml white wine
2 pints/1.2 litres red wine
sugar to taste
1 orange
may blossoms

Mix the wines in a bowl and add sugar to taste. Slice the orange thinly and add to the bowl. Cover the wine with well-washed may flowers cut off their stalks. Cover well and leave until the next day. This drink was served, well chilled, to May Day visitors, but now that this day falls on 1 May, when the tree is unlikely to be in flower, an excuse should be made for another celebration later on in the month; for it is such a festive and cheerful cup, and as pretty as springtime itself.

May Liqueur

may flowers
2 tbsps sugar
$\frac{1}{2}$ bottle brandy

Cut the flowers from their sprays and loosely pack them into a wide-necked bottle. Add the sugar and shake up together well. Fill the bottle up with brandy, cork and store in a warm place for 6 months, shaking during the first few weeks to dissolve the sugar. Strain and bottle in a small container.

May Blossom Wine
✸

This well-known country wine can be made following the instructions for flower wines on page 222.

Hawthorn Leaves   (Spring)

Chop the young leaves and leaf buds and add them to summer salads – they are particularly good in potato or beetroot salads. Alternatively, make sandwiches with them. They have a lovely nutty taste.

Hawthorn Roulade
✸

I tried this out on my dubious little daughter and her even more dubious friend: where were the fish fingers, they wondered? Ten minutes later there was no roulade left and I thought I had made enough for four!

> 4 oz/100 g plain flour
> 1 tsp salt
> $\frac{1}{2}$ tsp baking powder
> 2 oz/50 g shredded suet
> a handful of young hawthorn leaves

Make a suet crust by sifting the flour, salt and baking powder, adding the suet and mixing to a dough with a little water. Knead well until it is light, then roll out about $\frac{1}{2}$ inch/1 cm thick in a long narrow shape.

Wash and dry the leaves, chop them finely and press them into the crust. Moisten the edges and roll up, pressing the edges together to seal the roulade.

Bake at 425°F/220°C or gas mark 7 for 35 minutes and serve hot with gravy or tomato sauce. Serves 4, if you are lucky, otherwise 2 or 3.

As a variation, try adding finely chopped spring onions and slivers of lean bacon to the leaves before rolling up the crust.

Hawthorn Berries (Autumn)

Haws are another example, along with the elderberry, of an abundant and widespread fruit which is much under-used. They have a marvellous flavour and it is well worth trying them out in the following recipes.

Hawthorn berry

Haw Sauce
❧

1½ lb/750 g haws
¾ pint/450 ml vinegar
4 oz/100 g sugar
1 oz/25 g salt
1 tsp freshly ground black pepper

Strip the berries off their sprays and wash them. Put into a pan with the vinegar and cook over a gentle heat for 30 minutes. Press the pulp through a sieve and return to the pan with the sugar and seasonings. Boil for 10 minutes. Bottle and seal.

This makes a delicious ketchup to go with rich meats, either hot or cold.

Jellies Made with Haws
❧

Following the recipe on page 63 for making crab-apple jelly, try these combinations. Made with haws alone, the jelly is very thick, and the mixtures make a better consistency.

1. Haw and pear jelly (equal quantities of fruit).

2. Haw and apple jelly (equal quantities of fruit).

3. Haw and crab-apple jelly (equal quantities of fruit).

They all make delicious savoury jellies to go with roasts, poultry or cold dishes.

Hawthorn Berry Wine

Wine can be made from haws (see Bibliography, Books Recommended for Wine-Making, page 238).

Hogweed

(*Cow Parsnip*)

Summer

Heracleum sphondylium.
Umbelliferae family.
Native biennial, very common.
Height: up to 5 feet/1.75 m.
Flowers (white) June to August.

The young shoots are very tasty when boiled and eaten with melted butter.

Hop   (PLATE IV)

Spring and early summer

Humulus lupulus.
Cannabiaceae family.
Native perennial, common in England
and Wales.
Climbs high into hedges.
Flowers (cream) July to August.

The young shoots of the hop (known to the French as *jets d'houblon*) have been eaten as a vegetable since the sixteenth century, particularly in France.

Boil the hop tops – the top four leaves – in salted water or stock until tender and serve with melted butter. Cooked *al dente* and eaten with the fingers, like asparagus, they are a treat in their own right.

Alternatively, toss the cooked tops in butter and add a little cream (*à l'anversoise*), or serve them cold with vinaigrette – they make a delicious salad.

Tea can be made with the leaves of hops (see page 196).

Hop Sauce
✤

Parboil the shoots in salted water or stock, drain and chop. Mix with softened butter, season to taste and serve with fish or chicken.

Hop Top Soup
✤

> 1 lb/500 g lentils
> 3 pints/1.8 litres stock or water
> salt
> 1 large onion
> olive oil
> 3 handfuls hop tops
> cream

Soak the lentils. Cook in the water or stock until soft (about an hour) and season as necessary.

Chop the onion finely and cook until soft in the oil. Add the chopped hop tops and cook until the leaves are tender but not soft. Add to the lentil base and heat through. Season to taste, finish with cream and serve immediately. For 6.

Horseradish (PLATE IV)

Summer

Armoracia rusticana.
Cruciferae family.
Introduced perennial, common in the
south east.
Height: up to 3 feet/1 m.
Flowers (white) May to June.

The young leaves of this vigorous plant can be chopped and eaten in salads but it is the root that is most widely used. Dig the root, scrub it well but don't peel it since the tastiest part is the outside and not the core. Scrape slivers from it with a sharp knife, or grate it. This is an eye-watering exercise but you needn't do very much of it as a little horseradish goes a long way.

Basic Horseradish Sauce

Dig a root, scrub it and grate it or cut off slivers with a sharp knife. Mix with vinegar, white sugar and cream, to taste, and use it to accompany smoked fish or spread it on slices of ham and roll them up for canapés.

Grated horseradish can also be added to softened butter to serve with poached or grilled fish, or try adding it to tomato juice instead of Worcestershire sauce.

Horseradish and Walnut Sauce

3 oz/75 g walnuts
1 tbsp basic horseradish sauce (see
    above)
1 tbsp breadcrumbs
1 tsp wine vinegar
1 small carton double cream, whipped

Blanch the nuts and grind them in the blender, and mix with the rest of the ingredients. This sauce is excellent with smoked fish and also with cold cooked root vegetables such as celeriac, beetroot and carrots.

It also makes a very good filling for an avocado, and goes well with salt beef.

Horseradish Croustades

    round bread rolls and the same number
      of eggs
    chopped cow parsley leaves, dandelion,
      marjoram and garlic
    basic horseradish sauce (see above)
    1 oz/25 g grated cheese per roll
    salt and pepper
    softened butter

Cut the rolls in half and scoop out the soft insides. Mix the herbs, horseradish, cheese and seasonings with enough butter to bind, and spread over the insides of the rolls. Break eggs into half of them, season and dot with butter. Bake them all in a buttered baking dish at 400°F/200°C or gas mark 6 until the eggs are just set. Serve at once with the empty halves replaced on top.

Beetroot with Horseradish

    1 lb/500 g cooked beetroot
    2 oz/50 g butter
    salt
    2 tsps grated horseradish
    1 small carton single cream

Slice the beetroot very finely. Melt the butter and heat the beetroot through, turning it gently with a wooden spoon. Add the salt and the horseradish, and then the cream. Stir until well mixed together and heated through. Serve at once.

Salads with Horseradish

1. Apple and Horseradish

Grate some eating apples and an equal quantity of carrots. Add some grated horseradish root and dress with sour cream or yoghurt and lemon juice. Sprinkle with fresh herbs and serve.

2. Potato and Beetroot Salad

Boil waxy new potatoes in their skins until tender. Slice while they are still warm. Cook tiny fresh beetroot in their skins and, when cool, peel and quarter them. Dress the vegetables with mayonnaise to which you have added some grated horseradish and finely chopped parsley.

3. Sausage Salad

Cook some frankfurters and cut them into rounds. Dice some Gruyère cheese, shred some crisp young lettuce and dress with a horseradish dressing made of grated horseradish added to cream and seasoned with lemon juice.

Horseradish Cheese Spread

2 oz/50 g butter
4 oz/100 g cream cheese
fresh tarragon
grated horseradish
salt and pepper
1 tsp double cream

Mash the butter and the cheese until well blended. Chop the tarragon and add to the cheese. Add horseradish to taste, season and thin out a little with the cream.

Serve on cheese crackers or celery. Thinned out with more cream, you can use this as a cocktail dip.

Horseradish Vinegar

1 shallot
1 quart/1 litre white distilled vinegar
¼ lb/100 g grated horseradish
salt

Chop the shallot and add to the vinegar in a pan. Heat to just below simmering point, then add the horseradish and season. Cover tightly and heat gently for 20 minutes. Leave to stand for a week. Strain and re-boil hard. Bottle while still hot. This is very good with fish and chips.

Pickled Horseradish

Scrub the roots and grate them. Pack loosely into jars and cover with salted vinegar (1 tsp salt per ½ pint/300 ml vinegar). Use within eighteen months.

Preserved Horseradish

Scrub the roots, cut them into slices and dry them in a very slow oven until brittle. Then pound them in a mortar and store in airtight jars. Horseradish keeps its flavour extremely well when preserved in this way, and will keep indefinitely.

Japonica

(Japanese Quince)

Summer

Chaenomeles japonica.
Rosaceae family.
Deciduous dwarf shrub from Japan.
Height: up to 3 feet/90 cm; spread: about
5 to 7 feet/1.5 to 2 m.
Flowers (orange blossoms) March to
May.
Fruits irregularly with fragrant yellow
apple-scented fruits in August.

Although not, strictly speaking, a hedgerow plant, this is a common garden shrub whose fruits are well worth using.

Japonica Jam
✿

4 lb/2 kg japonica fruits
6 pints/3 litres water
sugar
2 tsps ground cloves

Slice the fruit and simmer in the water until tender. Sieve, pressing the pulp through well, and weigh the resulting liquid. Add an equal quantity of sugar and stir together over a low heat until dissolved. Bring to the boil, add the cloves and boil hard to setting point. Pot and seal. (See Jam-Making on page 226.)

Some jams using sweeter fruits require less sugar. The general rule for making jams is to use ¾ lb/325 g to each 1 lb/500 g of cooked fruit.

A jelly can also be made with japonica fruits following the method for crab-apple jelly (see page 63). To every 2 lb/1 kg japonica fruit add 4 tablespoons lemon juice.

Juniper (PLATE V)

Autumn

Juniperus communis.
Cupressaceae family.
Native shrub found on heaths, moorland,
chalk downs and in birch or pine woods.
Fairly common: most widespread in
Scotland.
Height: up to 16 feet/5 m.
Fruits (black with a bluish bloom)
September to October. The berries take 2
to 3 years to ripen. Always blue-black,
they finally grow to about $\frac{1}{2}$ cm ($\frac{1}{4}$ inch)
across and are no softer than a sloe.

It is well worth harvesting these luscious-looking berries and drying them for their unique and pungent flavour, because they are an expensive item on the grocery list. In the old days juniper was a traditional flavouring in English cookery and was used especially in the spicing of meats. The berries give a wonderful flavour to pâtés and stuffings – try adding them to a stuffing for boned shoulder of pork, or pound a few berries in a mortar with some salt, mix with olive oil and serve on gammon rashers. Their best-known use is in flavouring gin – wild crops are harvested in Italy and Yugoslavia and imported to distillers in this country.

The smoke from burning juniper was thought to keep off demons and was therefore burned during outbreaks of plague. To cut down or to dream about a juniper was unlucky, but on the other hand to dream about its berries brought good fortune as it was believed to prophesy the birth of a child.

To dry the berries, put them in a slow oven with the door ajar until they have shrivelled a little. Store them in small airtight jars. They can be used, apart from anything else, to make tea (see Teas on page 196); crush them slightly before infusing them.

Juniper Conserve

juniper berries
water
sugar

Cook the berries gently in water to cover until soft but not broken. Sieve them, then add three times their weight in sugar and dissolve over a low heat. Boil for a few minutes until thick, then pot and seal. Children love this preserve on bread and butter, and it also makes an original garnish for cold meats.

Juniper Butter

3 tbsps very finely chopped onion
4 tbsps melted butter
1 tsp crushed garlic
6–10 juniper berries, crushed
lemon juice
parsley
salt and pepper

Cook the chopped onion gently in the butter until soft, then add the garlic. Remove from the heat and add the juniper berries, lemon juice and parsley. Season and chill. Serve on grilled fish.

Juniper Potatoes

1 lb/500 g potatoes
2 oz/50 g butter
salt and pepper
8 juniper berries

Peel and grate the potatoes. Soak in cold water, drain and dry well in a towel. Melt the butter in a heavy pan and add the potatoes. Turn until covered with butter and, as they begin to soften, season well and add the crushed juniper berries. Cook, covered with a lid, over the lowest possible heat, well pressed down in the pan, for about ¾ hour or until crisp and brown underneath. Turn out on a hot plate and serve. For 3 or 4.

Veal with Juniper

1 oz/25 g butter
2 escalopes of veal, well-seasoned
2 onions
1 clove of garlic
4 juniper berries
salt and pepper
2 oz/50 g Gruyère cheese
breadcrumbs

Melt the butter and sauté the veal lightly. Set aside. Add the finely chopped onions and crushed garlic to the butter and cook gently until soft. Add the crushed berries and seasonings. Put this mixture on the bottom of a baking dish, lay the veal on top, season and cover with slices of Gruyère. Sprinkle with breadcrumbs and bake at 375°F/190°C or gas mark 5 for 10 to 15 minutes. For 2.

Lady's Mantle

Spring and summer

Alchemilla vulgaris.
Rosaceae family.
Native perennial of grass verges and
woodland. Common, especially in the
north.
Height: up to 14 inches/35 cm.
Flowers (yellow) May to September.

Apart from being a constituent of Easter ledger pudding (see page 16), an infusion of the leaves in hot water should be taken – according to Culpeper – as a drink by ladies who have difficulty in conceiving (see Teas on page 196): alchemy at work, as indicated by its generic name. A pillow filled with the dried leaves of lady's mantle is said to induce sleep.

Lady's Smock

Spring

Cardamine pratensis.
Cruciferae family.
Native perennial, common in meadows
and near streams.
Height: up to 21 inches/55 cm.
Flowers (pink) April to July.

When daisies pied and violets blue
And lady-smocks all silver white
And cuckoo buds of yellow hue
Do paint the meadows with delight,
The cuckoo then, on every tree,
Mocks married men; for thus sings he,
Cuckoo, cuckoo, cuckoo: o word of fear,
Unpleasing to a married ear.

William Shakespeare, *Love's Labour's Lost*

This wild flower is one of the first to appear in the early spring and is a member of the cabbage family. The leaves contain valuable minerals and also vitamin C, and they have a hot cress-like flavour. They can be used in green or mixed salads or in herb butters and sauces. Try them as a constituent of an *omelette fines herbes*: but don't bring the whole plant into the house – to do so will bring bad luck as it is a plant of the fairies.

Laver

see Seaweeds, page 179

Lime (Common)

(Linden)

Spring and summer

Tilia vulgaris.
Tiliaceae family.
Hardy, fast-growing natural hybrid.
Likes full sun or semi-shade.
Height: up to 39 m (130 feet).
Leaves bright green and smooth, often
covered with resin.
Flowers (creamy yellow) in drooping
clusters of 4 to 10 in early July.
Fruits (pea-sized), usually one-seeded, in
autumn.

The soft young leaves of the linden tree, picked in the early spring, are delicious in sandwiches. Remove the stalks, wash and dry them, chop them, sprinkle with a little salt and put between slices of fresh, buttered bread. Or mix the chopped leaves with a little cream cheese to spread on crackers.

Lime Flowers

These pretty yellow flowers can be dried and used to make a fragrant tea, known in France as *tilleul* and highly esteemed for its digestive properties. (See instructions for making teas on page 196.)

The flowers can also be made into fritters and served sprinkled with sugar (for the fritter batter, see page 53).

Lime Blossom Wine

A delicate wine can be made using lime flowers (see Bibliography, Books Recommended for Wine-Making, page 238, and Flower Wines, page 222).

Mallow (Common) (PLATE V)

Summer

Malva sylvestris.
Malvaceae family.
Native perennial, very common.
Height: up to 20 inches/50 cm.
Flowers (pink-purple) June to
September.

The young leaves of this well-known wild flower are rich in vitamins and have a strong, distinctive taste which is rich and slightly bitter. They can be boiled and eaten with butter as a side vegetable, or added to brown rice or to savoury vegetable dishes for flavouring.

Deep Fried Mallow

Wash the young leaves and dry them thoroughly. Deep-fry in vegetable oil at 375°F/190°C until they are crisp and curly. Drain well on kitchen paper, sprinkle with salt and serve at once.

Mallow Soup

2 large handfuls mallow leaves
2 tbsps olive oil
2 medium onions
4 cloves garlic
6 coriander seeds
a little flour
¾ pint/450 ml chicken stock
salt and pepper
cream

Wash and chop the leaves. Heat the oil gently and add the chopped onions. Cook, covered, over a low heat until soft, adding the crushed garlic and pounded coriander seeds after a few minutes. Sprinkle with a little flour and stir until it is absorbed. Add the stock, stirring while the soup thickens. Bring to the boil and add the leaves. Simmer for 10 to 15 minutes and then liquidize. Season to taste and add a pinch of sugar if required. Add cream to finish, re-heat and serve. For 2–3.

Marigold

Summer

Calendula officinalis.
Compositae family.

> Here's flowers for you;
> Hot lavender, mints, savory, marjoram;
> The marigold, that goes to bed i' the sun,
> And with him rises weeping.
>
> William Shakespeare, *A Winter's Tale*

In *A Niewe Herball* of 1578, Dodoens-Lyte says of the marigold: 'It has pleasant, bright and shining yellow flowers, the which do close at the setting downe of the sunne, and do spread and open againe at the sunne rising.' It is such an abundant grower in any garden that it seems a shame not to use the petals – they give a saffron flavouring and colouring to rice dishes, and can be used in fish soups or stews, either fresh or dried. Indeed, Gerard goes so far as to say 'that no broths are well made without dried Marigolds'. They have a spicy taste and make an attractive garnish for salads as well as making a refreshing tea (see page 196). The young leaves can be eaten in salads, too.

Marigold and Crab Hors d'œuvre

> 1 small lettuce
> 1 bunch watercress
> vinaigrette
> 1 crab
> 1 hard-boiled egg
> a few slices of cucumber
> marigold petals

Make a bed of shredded lettuce and watercress, well-dressed with vinaigrette. Put the crab meat on top. Garnish with slices of hard-boiled egg and cucumber and sprinkle liberally with marigold petals. Serves 4.

Marigold Savoury

An old Worcestershire recipe, to serve with pork.

> oil pastry (see page 224), using
>   6 oz/150 g flour
> 2 cooking apples
> 2 eggs
> a little top of the milk
> salt, pepper, thyme and sage
> 1 cup marigold petals

Line an 8-inch/20-cm pie dish with the pastry. Peel and core the apples and slice them very thinly. Cover the pastry with the slices and cook at 350°F/180°C or gas mark 4 until they are very soft. Beat the eggs, milk, seasonings and petals together, pour over the apples and cook until set – about 20 or 25 minutes. Serves 6.

Marigold Cream Cheese

> a handful of marigold petals
> 1 pint/600 ml milk
> a few drops of rennet
> salt

Put the rinsed chopped petals into the milk and add the rennet. When the milk has curdled, place it in a cloth napkin which has been wrung out in cold water. Sprinkle with salt, tie up as tightly as possible and hang it up to drip for a few hours.

When it has stopped dripping, squeeze it, shape it with a butter pat and leave for 24 hours before eating.

Marigold Buns

4 oz/100 g flour
a pinch of salt
2 oz/50 g butter
2 oz/50 g sugar
1 tsp baking powder
2 tbsps marigold petals
1 egg
milk

Sift the flour with the salt. Rub in the butter lightly, add the sugar and the baking powder and mix in the marigold petals. Beat the egg thoroughly and add to the mixture with a little milk to moisten it to a dough. Knead until light.

Grease individual bun tins, put 1 tablespoonful of the mixture into each one and bake at 450°F/230°C or gas mark 8 for 12 minutes.

Marigold Conserve

1 oz/25 g marigold petals
juice of ½ a lemon
2 oz/50 g sugar

Liquidize all the ingredients until thoroughly amalgamated. Pot in a small jar and use – yes, this is an Elizabethan recipe and here is what it says – as a cure for melancholy!

Marigold Wine

A flower wine can be made using marigolds (see Bibliography, Books Recommended for Wine–Making, page 238, and Flower Wines, page 222).

Marjoram

Summer

Origanum vulgare.
Labiatae family.
Common in dry hedgerows, roadsides and
pasture in England and Wales.
Height: up to 8 inches/20 cm.
Flowers (pink) July to September.

Wild marjoram is particularly good for flavouring meat dishes. Try roasting a chicken with a few sprigs of marjoram inside. It has a delicate and appetizing fragrance and also makes a very good addition to salads. The dried leaves can be made into a tea (see page 196).

Marjoram Olives

Wash some sprigs of marjoram and put them into a jar of good olive oil. Soak black olives in it for a day or two, covered tightly. They take on the taste of the marjoram and are simply delicious.

Marjoram Butter

Wash and chop some marjoram leaves finely and mash them into some softened butter. Season with a little salt and pepper. Serve with boiled onions. Alternatively, you can spread this on the bread of chicken sandwiches, or serve it with baked potatoes.

Marjoram Dumplings

8 oz/250 g stale bread
1 onion
olive oil
marjoram, parsley and thyme
salt, pepper and nutmeg
2 eggs
stock

Soak the bread in water, squeeze it dry and mash it. Cook the finely chopped onion gently in oil until soft, then add the chopped herbs. Mix well and add to the bread. Season to taste, beat the eggs, add to the mixture and stir well.

Drop egg-sized rounds of the mixture into the simmering stock and cook until puffed. Serve with fried onions to accompany roast or boiled meats.

Marjoram Potatoes

2 lb/1 kg potatoes
2 oz/50 g butter
marjoram, chopped parsley and
   tarragon
salt
¼ pint/150 ml sour cream
¼ pint/150 ml yoghurt

Peel the potatoes and cut them into small dice. Toss in melted butter over a medium heat until golden. Add the herbs and mix well, then season and add the sour cream and the yoghurt. Bake in a greased fireproof dish at 375°F/190°C or gas mark 5 for 1 hour. Serves 4.

Braised Chicory with Marjoram

1 lb/500 g chicory
butter
a good handful of chopped fresh
   marjoram
salt and pepper

Cut the chicory into rounds about ½ inch/1 cm thick and blanch in boiling water for 8 minutes. Line a buttered baking dish with alternate layers of chicory and marjoram. Season each layer and dot with butter as you go along. Bake, covered, at 300°F/150°C or gas mark 2 for 1½ hours.

Marjoram Jelly

Using 1 lb/500 g cooking apples to a large bunch of marjoram and a few slivers of lemon rind, make the jelly following the method for crab-apple jelly (page 63), cooking the herb with the apples.

Marjoram Scones

Marjoram becomes slightly sweet when it is dried and makes very good herb scones.

> 2 oz/50 g lard or margarine
> 4 oz/100 g flour
> a pinch of salt
> 2 tsps baking powder
> dried marjoram (about 2–3 tsps)
> milk

Rub the fat into the flour sifted with the salt. Add the baking powder and dried marjoram and mix to a dough with a little milk. Knead until light, roll out about ½ inch/1 cm thick and cut rounds with a scone-cutter or glass. Bake on a greased baking tray for 10 to 12 minutes at 450°F/230°C or gas mark 8. Makes 10 scones.

Marsh Thistle

Summer

Cirsium palustre.
Compositae family.
Native biennial of marshes, damp ground,
grassland and woods.
Common.
Height: up to 5 feet/1.5 m.

The young stems of the marsh thistle can be picked and peeled, and the inner stalks boiled and eaten with butter or used raw in salads.

Meadowsweet

Summer

Filipendula ulmaria.
Rosaceae family.
Native perennial, common in wet
meadows and marshes and on riverbanks.
Height: up to 8 inches/20 cm.
Flowers (creamy-white) June to August.

The young leaves of this lacy-looking wild flower give an aromatic and refreshing almond flavour to summer soups.

The flowers and leaves can be dried and infused to make a tea which has the same effect as aspirin (for the method, see page 196).

Wine can also be made from meadowsweet flowers in the same way as from other wild flowers. Make it according to the instructions for flower wines on page 222.

Medlar

Autumn

Mespilus germanica.
Rosaceae family.
Found naturalized in the hedgerows,
mostly in England.
Height: up to 10 feet/3 m.
Fruits (tan) September to October.

This small thorny tree with its large leaves is not often found in great abundance, and rarely fruits heavily in the wild. Medlars need to be kept for a few weeks after picking as they seldom ripen on the tree, and they soften during the storing period.

Baked Medlars
❧

Arrange the softened medlars on a baking dish and cover with knobs of butter, sugar and cloves. Bake for 10 minutes at 375°F/190°C or gas mark 5. Serve with cream.

Medlar Jelly
❧

Make following the recipe for crab-apple jelly on page 63.

Medlar Jam
❧

Make following the recipe for japonica jam on page 116.

Medlar Cheese
❧

Make following the recipe for blackberry cheese on page 22.

Mint

Summer

Labiatae family

There are more than a dozen types of mint growing wild in Britain; the following are the most commonly found:

Corn Mint
Mentha arvensis

Water Mint
Mentha aquatica

Pennyroyal
Mentha pugelium

Spearmint
Mentha spicata

Whorled Mint
Mentha verticillata

All these wild mints can be used in the same ways as the common garden variety (*Mentha viridis*) and the crystallized leaves (see page 95) of all of them make a lovely garnish for mousses, ices and cakes.

'The smell of mint, saith Pliny, doth stir up the minde, and the taste to a greedy desire for meate' (Gerard).

Mint Butter

1 tbsp chopped mint
2 oz/50 g butter
salt, pepper and lemon juice

Wash and chop the mint finely and mix with the softened butter. Season to taste and spread on the bread for cold lamb sandwiches.

Mint Cream Cheese

Mix chopped mint with cream cheese and serve as an original addition to the cheese board.

Mint in Salads

Chopped mint leaves are good in a variety of salads – cole slaw, celery and orange – or in a salad of cold cooked vegetables such as beetroot, cauliflower and French beans.

Add chopped mint to yoghurt and use as a dressing, or try making the following mint dip, which also makes a delicious garnish for summer soups.

Mint Dip

$\frac{1}{2}$ cucumber
salt
1 large clove of garlic
1 tbsp chopped mint
1 small carton yoghurt

Peel and grate the cucumber. Sprinkle it with salt and let it stand for a while. Drain off the liquid. Crush the garlic and add it with the mint and cucumber to the yoghurt. Season to taste.

Mint Vinegar

✲

Steep whole mint sprigs for 3 days in white wine vinegar, discarding the old ones daily and replacing with new ones.

Mint Jelly

✲

Make as for marjoram jelly on page 129.

Mint Tea

✲

See instructions for making teas on page 196.

Mushrooms (PLATE VIII)

The mystery of the mushroom is that it is neither a plant nor an animal: a fungus is a creature of its own unique category, although it is now generally classified as a primitive plant. Mushrooms contain no chlorophyll and cannot therefore manufacture their own food, so they live off other organic matter, either rotting matter (the saprophytes) or living matter (the parasites). There are thought to be about 40,000 species of fungi in the world, over 2000 of which are edible but most of which go to waste unpicked. Throughout Europe and in the Far East, particularly Japan, there is a thriving mushroom industry, and general knowledge of wild fungi is far more highly developed there than it is in this country: yet in Britain there grow 5000 species, over 200 of which are edible, and we choose to ignore this valuable and delicious source of food.

The great majority of people in Britain, although eager consumers of the cultivated mushroom, are not initiated into the wonders of wild-mushroom gathering. This is largely through lack of information and education and there would seem to be enormous scope here for developing a fascinating and rewarding study. Discovering edible fungi and all about them is an adventure in itself and a pastime much under-indulged in by the timid British public. The French set us an admirable example and we should follow it: they have a centre of inspection at the main vegetable market in Paris for trade assignments as well as for amateur gatherers, and in country districts it is often the local chemist who is the expert with whom mushroom pickers check their finds.

Mushrooms have always been considered a great gastronomic speciality – the Romans called them 'food for the gods' – and they are also a highly nutritious food. Some are as rich in protein as meat or fish and possess large amounts of minerals such as iron, calcium and phosphorus. Many contain a variety of vitamins, notably the Bs and D_2.

There can, however, be only one rule of thumb about eating wild mushrooms – and that is, *if in doubt, don't*. Some species of mushrooms are poisonous and can cause death in a particularly painful manner, so never take any risks: always check your mushrooms carefully before you eat them. Pick only the young specimens in all cases, since ageing fungi can produce unpleasant symptoms, and always eat them as fresh as possible.

Arm yourself with one or several of the books recommended on page 237 and sally forth into the fields and woods: you will find the pleasures of mushroom hunting engrossing, rewarding and very enjoyable.

Here as a guideline for beginners are The Safe Seven: examples of unmistakable wild mushrooms common throughout Britain which offer highly satisfactory culinary rewards.

The Safe Seven

1. Morel (*Morchella esculenta*).*
2. Puffballs (*Lycoperdon perlatum* and *Calvatia gigantea*).
3. Field Mushroom (*Agaricus campestris*).
4. Cep (*Boletus edulis*).
5. Chanterelle (*Cantharellus cibarius*).
6. Wood Hedgehog (*Hydnum repandum*).
7. Oyster Mushroom (*Pleurotus ostreatus*).

1. Morel (Morchella esculenta)

The morel has a shrivelled, honeycombed appearance and varies in colour from tan to rich brown. It grows 2 to 6 inches/5 to 15 cm high, the stalk often being shorter than the cap. It is found in clusters or rings in woods and on grassland, particularly in clearings on sandy soil in the south and east of England. It appears in spring from April to June but is an elusive mushroom as it seldom appears consecutively in the same place.

It is a gastronomic treat and much sought after by gourmets for its unique flavour. It requires longer cooking than the cultivated mushroom, and is very good stewed in butter or poached in cream. It is delicious *aux fines herbes* or cooked in a light curry sauce. It has a fine mealy texture which makes it a marvellous addition to salads.

2. Puffballs

(a) Common Puffball (Lycoperdon perlatum)

This mushroom grows 3 to 5 inches/7 to 13 cm tall and $1\frac{1}{2}$ inches/4 cm

---

*The scientific names of the fungi are those given in S. Nilsson and O. Persson, *Fungi of Northern Europe*, Vols. I and II (Penguin Books, 1978).

across. It is pear- or fig-shaped and covered with conical warts. It is white at first, turning brownish as it grows older, and has a smell rather like a radish. Pick it when the flesh is young and white, before the spores turn brown and powdery. It is to be found in open fields and under rotting logs or among fallen leaves and is common in beech woods from June to November.

It makes a delicious creamed purée as well as being very tasty in salads.

(b) Giant Puffball (Calvatia gigantea)

This is smooth and pure white when young and edible and grows in meadows, pastures and heaths. It can grow to 20 inches/½ m or more in diameter, and weigh anything from 6 to 20 lb/3 to 10 kg. The inside is spongy and white, but don't eat it once it starts to yellow. As it ages, it will turn olive-brown. It grows from May to October.

It is excellent cut into slices about ½ inch/1 cm thick, dipped into egg and breadcrumbs and fried in butter as a mushroom cutlet – or puffball steak as it is sometimes known.

3. Field Mushroom (Agaricus campestris)

This is the wild version of the cultivated mushroom and grows in rings or clusters from summer to autumn in all kinds of grassland and fields – from lowlands to mountain pastures – from July to October. The white cap measures 2 to 4 inches/5 to 10 cm across and the stem, which has a ring, is 1 to 3 inches/3 to 7 cm high. The gills are separate from the stem and are white at first, turning pinkish-grey and then purplish-brown with age. It has an excellent flavour and is good in all mushroom recipes. A word of warning: at its button stage it looks very similar to *Amanita verna* which is fatally poisonous, so pick it after it has opened out!

4. Cep (Boletus edulis)

The cep looks like a shiny well-baked bun with its distinctive round brown cap. It measures 4 to 8 inches/10 to 20 cm across and has a stout beige stem about 6 to 8 inches/15 to 20 cm tall. The flesh is white when young and edible and has a nutty taste. It has no gills but a mass of tubes on the underside of the cap which are best removed before cooking. It grows from

June to October in woods, usually with chestnuts, oaks and pines.

It has a beautiful flavour and dries extremely well for winter casseroles and soups. When fresh, cook in butter or cream, make a purée with it or cook in croustades (see page 141). It is delicious in an omelette or as a garnish for eggs. Try serving it in a curry sauce or *à la lyonnaise* (see page 142). Perhaps it is at its best *à la béarnaise* (see page 142).

5. *Chanterelle*   (Cantharellus cibarius)

The cap of this dramatic-looking mushroom is convex at first and then turns into a funnel shape with a wavy margin. It is $1\frac{3}{4}$ to 3 inches/4 to 7.5 cm across and has a short thick stem about 2 to 4 inches/5 to 10 cm high. It smells of apricots and its yellow flesh has a nutty taste. It is found growing in rings or clusters in birch, beech or fir woods, often among moss and grass, and on trodden ground beside paths or roads, from June to November. It makes excellent eating although it requires longer cooking than the cultivated mushroom.

6. *Wood Hedgehog*   (Hydnum repandum)

The cap of the wood hedgehog is 2 to 4 inches/5 to 10 cm across and is an irregular wavy shape with a smooth, dry, creamy-yellow surface. It has pale spines that turn brownish-yellow and a short fat stem about 1 to 3 inches/2 to 7 cm tall. The flesh of this common fungus is firm but fragile and has a delicate flavour – as with all wild mushrooms, eat it young. It grows in fairy rings in beech woods from July to November and is excellent in all the following recipes for mushrooms.

7. *Oyster Mushroom*   (Pleurotus ostreatus)

This looks like a shell with an uncurled edge and it varies in colour from olive green to grey or brown. Its cap is 2 to 5 inches/5 to 12 cm across and it has a short thick stem about $\frac{1}{2}$ to $1\frac{1}{2}$ inches/1 to 4 cm tall. Its flesh is soft and white. It grows clustered in tiers on deciduous trees, especially on old poplars, and on stumps and gateposts. It is abundant from October to December and makes marvellous fritters, soups and risottos; but do use the young ones – the older ones are tough and indigestible. They dry very well for winter casseroles.

Mushrooms with Anchovy Cream

8 oz/250 g mushrooms
butter
4 rounds of fried bread
6 anchovy fillets
4 tbsps cream
salt and pepper

Slice the mushrooms finely and cook them gently in butter. Put them on to the rounds of fried bread and keep hot. Chop the anchovies and mix them with the cream and seasonings. Heat through and place a spoonful of the mixture over each portion. Serve at once. For 4.

Grilled Mushrooms with Bacon

Grill flat mushrooms smooth side up with a little knob of butter on each one. When well done, turn and cover the gills with thin strips of bacon. Cook until crisp and serve at once.

Surprise Mushrooms

8 large round mushrooms
butter
8 tomatoes
4 rashers of bacon
salt and pepper

Season the mushrooms (use ceps, puffballs or oyster mushrooms) and sauté in a little butter. Skin the tomatoes, hollow each one out and place a mushroom inside. Cover with a strip of bacon and bake at 375°F/190°C or gas mark 5 for 25 minutes. Serves 4.

Mushroom Tartlets

8 small pastry tartlet cases, baked blind
(see page 224)

> 8 mushrooms, large enough to fill the
>   cases (field, cep or puffball)
> salt and pepper
> garlic butter

Season the mushrooms, put into the pastry shells and bake for 10 minutes at 400°F/200°C or gas mark 6. Pour over them the melted garlic butter and serve immediately. For 4.

Stuffed Mushrooms

> 4 mushrooms per person
> 2 rashers of bacon per person
> butter
> garlic and basil
> Parmesan cheese
> salt and pepper
> croûtons

Remove the stalks and place the mushroom caps in a well-buttered baking dish. Slice the rashers into thin strips and cook until crisp in butter. Add the finely chopped stalks and cook until they are soft. Add more butter, and when it has melted add the crushed garlic and chopped basil. When softened, add a little Parmesan cheese and season to taste. Fill the caps with this mixture, dot with croûtons and bake at 400°F/200°C or gas mark 6 for 10 minutes.

Mushrooms in Cream

Wipe the mushrooms clean and slice them. Heat some thick cream in a pan, season with salt and pepper and poach the mushrooms until they are soft and cooked through. Serve piping hot. All the wild mushrooms benefit from this way of cooking – it brings out their flavour to the maximum.

Mushroom Croustades

Chop and simmer mushrooms in butter and add, with the pan juices, to a little *sauce à la crème* (see page 224) with a few drops of lemon juice. Scoop the insides out of small bread rolls, pour in the mushroom mixture and heat through thoroughly. Serve very hot.

Mushrooms à la Béarnaise
❀

Brush the mushrooms with olive oil and insert slivers of garlic into the caps. Grill for about 10 minutes or until cooked through. Serve on a hot plate with a mixture of breadcrumbs fried with parsley until both are crisp.

Mushrooms à la Bordelaise
❀

Clean and slice the mushroom caps and stew them in butter until tender, with a little lemon juice. At the end of the cooking time, turn the heat up a little and brown the mushrooms. For each 1 lb/500 g of fungi, add the chopped stalks, 2 teaspoons chopped shallots, 2 tablespoons fresh breadcrumbs and a teaspoon of fresh chopped parsley. Toss in a pan until hot and serve immediately.

Mushrooms à la Provençale
❀

As for *à la bordelaise* above, but substitute garlic for the shallots.

Mushrooms à la Lyonnaise
❀

Melt some butter and cook finely chopped onion in it gently until very soft. Cook the mushrooms in butter, add to the onions, sprinkle with lemon juice and parsley and serve.

Mushrooms with Scrambled Eggs and Anchovy
❀

Clean, slice and season some mushrooms with salt; put them into an earthenware baking dish and cover it with foil. Bake at 400°F/200°C or gas mark 6 for 15 minutes or until soft. (This way of cooking them retains the flavour marvellously well and is not so rich as cooking in butter.)

Make some creamy scrambled eggs and stir in some chopped anchovy

Plate I   *1 Alexanders, 2 Bullace, 3 Chickweed, 4 Bilberry, 5 Comfrey*

Plate II   *1 Red deadnettle, 2 Chamomile, 3 White deadnettle, 4 Fat hen, 5 Broad-leaved dock*

Plate III   *1 Ground elder, 2 Garlic mustard, 3 Guelder rose, 4 Clary*

Plate IV   1 Hawthorn, 2 Horseradish, 3 Hop, 4 Crab-apple

Plate V   1 Juniper, 2 Common mallow, 3 Greater plantain, 4 Wild garlic (or ramsons)

Plate VI *1 Rock samphire, 2 Marsh samphire, 3 Salad burnet, 4 Laver, 5 Sloe*

Plate VII   *1 Smooth sow thistle, 2 Tansy, 3 Common sorrel, 4 Yarrow, 5 Yellow rocket (or wintercress)*

Plate VIII   *1 Morel, 2 Field mushroom, 3 Chanterelle, 4 Cep, 5 Wood hedgehog,*
6 Oyster mushroom, 7 Common puffball, 8 Giant puffball

fillets. Put the mushrooms on to pieces of toast, heap the eggs on top and serve immediately.

Other Suggestions for Using Wild Mushrooms:

Mushrooms make wonderful fritters – for the fritter batter, see page 53 – and, to make them, follow the recipe for comfrey fritters on page 54. Alternatively, try them in a mushroom risotto, soufflé or omelette, in vol-au-vent cases or curried. One lovely way to cook them is in the following old-fashioned recipe:

Mushroom Pudding

8 oz/250 g flour
1 tsp salt
1 tsp baking powder
4 oz/100 g shredded suet
12 oz/350 g mushrooms
2 oz/50 g bacon
salt and pepper
water

Sift the flour with the teaspoon of salt and baking powder and mix in the suet. Mix to a dough with cold water and knead lightly. Line a greased pudding basin with two thirds of the pastry.

Chop the mushrooms and bacon and season well. Fill the pastry with the mixture, add a tablespoon or two of water and cover with the rest of the pastry. Cover the pudding basin with a lid or with foil, very securely, and steam for 2½ hours. Serves 4.

Mushroom Soup

2 oz/50 g butter
3 shallots
8 oz/250 g mushrooms
salt and pepper
1½ pints/1 litre stock
cream

Melt the butter and add the finely sliced shallots. Slice the mushrooms and add to the pan with some more butter if need be. Cover and cook slowly until they are cooked through. Season to taste. Stir in the stock, bring to the boil and season to taste again. Stir in the cream and serve. For 4.

Finally, here are some ideas for preserving mushrooms – for those halcyon days when there are actually *too many* mushrooms around to eat fresh all at once!

Dried Mushrooms
✲

Simply thread the mushrooms on a fine string with a darning needle and hang them in a warm dry place until they are brittle.

Potted Mushrooms
✲

Wipe the mushrooms clean and sprinkle with salt. Cook in butter (4 oz or 100 g butter to 3 pints or 1.8 litres mushrooms) with salt, mace and a dash of cayenne. When they are well cooked, drain off the liquid and pack into potting jars. Cover thickly with clarified butter (see page 225) and store in a cool dry place. They will keep for many weeks in the refrigerator.

Mushroom Catsup or Ketchup
✲

Put fresh wild mushrooms into a large earthenware dish and sprinkle with salt. Cover. Put in a warm place – for example, the top of the boiler. Add more mushrooms and salt daily while the season is at its height, pressing them down well, for a week or 10 days at a time.

Boil the mushrooms in their liquid and then strain. To every 2 pints/1.2 litres of liquid add 4 tablespoons whole black peppers, 3 to 5 blades of mace or $\frac{1}{4}$ nutmeg and 1 tablespoon allspice berries. Bring to the boil again, strain and bottle. It keeps for about 6 months.

Pickled Mushrooms

Wipe the mushrooms clean and sprinkle them with salt. Put them in a pan over a low heat to draw out the liquid. Drain and pour over them enough spiced vinegar (see page 28) to cover. Seal and store for up to a year.

Mushrooms in Brine

Wipe the mushrooms clean with a damp cloth dipped in salt.

For every 1 lb/500 g mushrooms, make a mixture of:

> 6 oz/175 g salt
> 1 oz/25 g sugar
> 1 pint/600 ml water
> 12 peppercorns

Boil the mixture for a few minutes, then add the mushrooms and stir for a few minutes. Bottle and store in a cool place for up to 6 months.

Nasturtium

(*Indian Cress*)

Summer

Tropaeolum majus.
Tropaeolaceae family.
Climbs 2 yards/1.8 m or more.
Flowers (orange trumpet shaped) 1½–2
inches/38–50 mm across in August. Non-
climbing cultivars from yellow to red.
Entire peltate leaves.
Fruits with round green seeds in early
autumn.

The leaves of this common garden flower have a spicy, slightly hot flavour. They are a good substitute for watercress and make delicious sandwiches. Pick the young, pale green leaves for a more delicate taste, and garnish any dishes you use them in with one or two of the brilliantly coloured flowers – they, and the seeds, have their uses too.

Nasturtium and Walnut Soup

2 large handfuls of young nasturtium
  leaves
1½ oz/40 g butter
2 oz/50 g walnuts
1 pint/600 ml stock
salt
cream

Wash, dry and chop the leaves. Cook in the melted butter over a low heat until they have wilted and turned dark green. Add the finely chopped walnuts and cook together for a few minutes. Add the stock, stirring well, and simmer for 10 minutes. Liquidize, thin out with more stock if necessary and season to taste. Finish with the cream.

Serve chilled, with a flower floating in the middle of each soup bowl. It is also excellent hot. Serves 2 or 3.

Nasturtium and Mushroom Casserole

> 2 handfuls of nasturtium leaves
> garlic
> olive oil
> 8 oz/250 g mushrooms
> salt, pepper and fresh thyme

Blanch the leaves for ½ minute in boiling water. Drain and dry. Crush a clove of garlic into the olive oil and brush each leaf with it. Slice the mushrooms and season them. Place a third of the leaves over the bottom of an oiled ovenproof dish, place half the mushrooms on the leaves, cover with the second third of the leaves, and repeat the layering. Brush the top layer of leaves with more garlic olive oil. Cover with foil and bake at 375°F/190°C or gas mark 5 for 20 minutes. Serve with toast fingers. For 2.

Nasturtium Leaf Rolls

Blanch young nasturtium leaves for ½ minute in boiling salted water. Drain and dry. Brush both sides of each leaf with olive oil, and place in the middle of each leaf a spoonful of either chopped chicken, turkey, ham, tuna or salmon salad. Roll up, tucking in the sides to make a parcel, and serve with mayonnaise.

Nasturtium Flower Sauce

> ½ pint/300 ml flowers, packed down
> 1 pint/600 ml vinegar
> 4 shallots
> 6 cloves of garlic
> salt and pepper
> soy sauce

Wash and dry the flowers. Boil the vinegar with the chopped shallots, garlic and seasonings for 10 minutes. Pour over the flowers while still hot.

Cover and store. After 3 months, strain the liquid and add soy sauce to taste. Bottle and store, and use instead of Worcestershire sauce.

Nasturtium Flower Vinegar

Gather the flowers when they are perfectly dry and put them into bottles with a little whole white pepper and mace.

Scald enough vinegar to fill the bottles and, when cold, pour it over the flowers, filling the bottles to the top.

Seal and store.

Pickled Nasturtium Seeds

Put the seeds into salted water (6 oz or 175 g salt per 1 quart or 1 litre water) and soak them overnight. Then wash and dry them and pack into little jars. Add a little grated horseradish if desired. Pour over them cold spiced vinegar (see page 28), cover and seal. Store for a few months before using as a substitute for capers, as in the sauces below.

Caper Sauce

Stir into 3 oz/75 g melted butter 3 or 4 tablespoonfuls of pickled nasturtium seeds (see above). Add a little of their vinegar and serve the sauce as soon as it boils.

Caper Sauce for Fish

1 oz/25 g pickled nasturtium seeds
2 oz/50 g butter
1 tbsp flour
1 tbsp vinegar
salt and pepper
½ pint/300 ml meat stock
1 tsp chopped parsley

Wash and chop the seeds. Heat the butter, add the flour and stir until smooth. Mix in the nasturtium seeds, vinegar, salt and pepper, stir in the stock and simmer for 10 minutes. Add the parsley and serve.

Nettle (Stinging)

Spring and summer

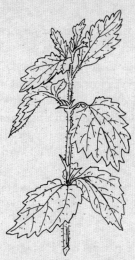

Urtica dioica.
Urticaceae family.
Native perennial, very common in woods,
ditches and grassy places.
Height: up to 5 feet/1.5 m.
Greenish-brown seedheads from May to
September.

At one time the nettlebed was a characteristic feature of an English country garden and highly treasured for its riches of protein, minerals and vitamins. Nettles were traditionally taken as a spring tonic in the form of soup or tea, as they were said to purify the blood – no doubt they did, too, being the first green vegetable to appear after the long winter's diet of salted meat. Their cultivation was part of a natural plant rotation and they were sold in eighteenth-century markets as a vegetable. Victorian cookbooks include nettles as a matter of course and it is only in recent years, in the hey-day of the supermarket, that they have been forgotten. They make a tasty vegetable and have the advantage of being available throughout the growing season. When cut back they re-grow vigorously within a few weeks. They have a quite different taste from the deadnettles (see page 72), from which they are easily distinguishable in that the stinging nettle does not have flowers. Blanched, they freeze extremely well.

To Pick and Cook Nettles

First put on a pair of rubber gloves! Pick the four top leaves of young nettles before they get straggly and go to seed. Wash them thoroughly and then cook them down in their own water, with salt, as you would for spinach. Boil for about 15 minutes and drain.

For a side vegetable, chop and season them, toss with a knob of butter or add to a little béchamel sauce or cream and sprinkle with croûtons.

Suggestions for Serving Cooked Nettles

Use them as a base for poached eggs and serve with triangles of fried bread, or bake an egg in a ramekin lined with buttered, cooked nettles.

As a salad, chop the drained nettles and leave to cool. Toss in vinaigrette and serve sprinkled with a little grated lemon rind.

Nettle Soup

> a large saucepan full of nettle tops
> 1½ oz/40 g butter
> 1 oz/25 g flour
> 1½ pints/1 litre stock
> salt and pepper
> croûtons

Cook the washed nettle tops (see above) in their own water with a little salt for 10 to 15 minutes. Drain and chop.

Melt the butter, add the flour and stir in the hot stock gradually, until the mixture thickens. Simmer for several minutes, then season to taste. Mix with the cooked nettles and liquidize. Thin out as necessary with more stock and finish with the cream. Serve with croûtons. For 4.

Nettle and Lentil Soup

Make this soup following the recipe for hop and lentil soup (hop top soup) on page 111, using nettle tops in place of hops.

Nettle and Oatmeal Soup

> 2 spring onions
> 1 oz/25 g butter
> 1½ oz/40 g fine oatmeal
> 1½ pints/1 litre milk or stock
> 1½ pints/1 litre nettle tops
> salt
> croûtons

Chop the onions finely and soften them in the melted butter. Sprinkle in the oatmeal and cook until it is golden. Add the liquid gradually, stirring all the time, then the washed nettle tops, and bring to the boil. Add the salt, simmer for 15 to 20 minutes, then liquidize and serve with croûtons. For 4.

Nettle and Comfrey Soup

Make as for nettle soup above, using equal quantities of cooked nettle tops and cooked comfrey.

Nettle Haggis

> 8 oz/250 g cooked nettle tops
> 2 leeks, chopped
> 4 oz/125 g cabbage, chopped
> 2 Spanish onions, chopped
> 6 oz/175 g lean bacon, chopped
> 8 oz/250 g oatmeal
> 8 oz/250 g suet
> salt, pepper and nutmeg
> a little stock

Mix the vegetables, bacon, oatmeal, suet and seasonings together and moisten with the stock. Put into a pudding basin and cover securely. Steam for 4 hours and serve with hot gravy. For 6.

Nettles with Almonds

> 1 pint/600 ml nettles, pressed down
> 2 tbsps olive oil
> salt and soy sauce
> 2 oz/50 g whole almonds

Wash the nettles and shake them dry. Cook gently in the oil until the leaves are wilted and dark – about 10 minutes. Then add salt and soy sauce to taste. Cook gently until tender (another 10 minutes or so).

Halve the almonds and roast them in the oven at 375°F/190°C or gas mark 5, until lightly browned. Mix with the nettles and serve immediately.

Champp

> 1 lb/500 g cooked potatoes
> ¼ pint/150 ml milk
> 6 spring onions
> ½ lb/250 g cooked nettle tops
> 2 oz/50 g butter

Mash the potatoes with the milk and stir in the chopped spring onions and nettle tops. Heat through thoroughly and put into a baking dish with a well in the centre. Fill with the melted butter and serve immediately.

Dip the champ into the melted butter as you eat: it is a wonderfully warming cold-weather dish and a very good way of using frozen blanched nettles during the winter.

Nettle Tea

Make a tea by infusing young nettle leaves in boiling water. Let it stand for 20 minutes and then re-heat. Strain and serve sweetened with honey. (See Teas and Tisanes on page 196.)

Nettle Beer

> 2 lb/1 kg young nettles
> 2 lemons
> 1 gallon/4 litres water
> 1 lb/500 g demerara sugar
> 1 oz/25 g cream of tartar
> ¾ oz/20 g fresh baker's yeast

Put the nettles in a saucepan with the thinly pared rind of the lemons. Pour on the water and bring to the boil. Simmer for 15 to 20 minutes. Strain on to the sugar and cream of tartar, stir well, then add the juice of the lemons and the yeast mixed with a little of the liquid. Cover and keep in a warm place for 3 days. Remove to a cool place for 2 days, then strain and bottle in screw-top cider bottles. Keep for a week before drinking.

Nettle Wine

A wine can be made using nettles (see Bibliography, Books Recommended for Wine-Making, page 238).

Oak

Summer and autumn

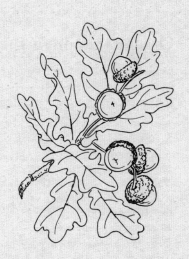

Quercus robur.
Fagaceae family.
Native and common.
Deciduous and very long-lived (up to 800 years or more).
Height: up to more than 100 feet/30 m.
Flowers (greenish brown) in May.
Fruits (acorns) 1¼ inch/3 cm long, ovoid, on long stalks, which ripen in October.
Leaves, sessile, dark green above, smooth below.

> If the oak's before the ash
> You will only get a splash,
> If the ash precedes the oak
> You will surely get a soak.
>
> Popular saying

Oak Leaf Wine

Wine can be made from oak leaves (see Bibliography, Books Recommended for Wine-Making, page 238).

Acorn Coffee

Acorns can be used as a coffee substitute when they are ripe and have fallen out of their cups. Chop the kernels finely and dry them in a slow oven until they are light brown. Grind them and return them to the oven again for a short time to dry further.

The 'coffee' is made in the usual way but lacks any stimulant effect since it contains no caffeine.

Orache (Common)

(*Iron-Root*)

Summer

Atriplex patula.
Chenopodiaceae family.
Native annual, common in England and
Wales, found in waste places, on
roadsides and cultivated land.
Height: up to 3 feet/1 m.
Flowers (green seed-heads) July to
September.

A close relative of fat hen, common orache can be used in the same ways (see pages 88–93). Also related are:

Frosted Orache (*Atriplex laciniata*), found at high tide marks on coasts around Britain.

Shore Orache (*Atriplex littoralis*), found on mud flats on the eastern coastline.

Spear-Leaved Orache (*Atriplex hastata*), common and widespread.

Parsley Piert

Spring and summer

Aphanes arvensis.
Rosaceae family.
Native annual, found on arable land.
Common and widespread.
Stems: up to 6 inches/15 cm.
Flowers (pale green) April to October.

Traditionally used to cure kidney stones, parsley piert is made into a pickle, and the Hebrideans eat it raw – it is as good an addition to salads as salad burnet (see page 171) when picked young in the early spring. It gets its name from the French words *perce-pierre*, meaning a plant which 'breaks through stony ground'.

Parsley Piert and Samphire Relish

8 oz/250 g parsley piert leaves
8 oz/250 g young samphire shoots,
    either rock or marsh (see page 173)
3 lb/1.5 kg green tomatoes
1 green and 1 red pepper
8 onions
2 cucumbers
salt
2 pints/1.2 litres malt vinegar
2 lb/1 kg sugar
2 tbsps each of flour and curry powder
1 tbsp mustard

Cut all the vegetables finely and sprinkle with the salt. Leave to stand, covered, overnight. Strain off most of the liquid.

Put the vegetable ingredients into a pan with the vinegar, sugar and salt. Bring to the boil and simmer for 1 hour. Blend the flour, curry powder and mustard with a little of the liquid from the pan to make a creamy paste and add it to the contents. Stir it in well and simmer for $\frac{1}{2}$ hour longer. Pot and seal.

Pine

Spring

Pinus sylvestris.
Pinaceae family.

Taken as an infusion in the spring, pine needle tea is said to cleanse the system. But one of the most luxurious ways of using the needles is to put them into a hot bath to make it smell beautiful.

Plantain (Greater) (PLATE V)

(Rat's Tail Plantain)

Summer

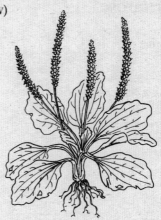

Plantago major.
Plantaginaceae family.
Common.
Height: up to 6 inches/15 cm.
Flowers (green-brown spikes) May to
September.

The young leaves of this persistent plant are excellent in salads and are rich in calcium and potassium. They contain vitamins K and C. Try cooking plantain like spinach and putting a poached egg on top of a bed of the boiled buttered leaves.

Plantain Salad

1 bunch of watercress
1 bunch of plantain leaves
½ cucumber
garlic
1 cold potato
vinaigrette

Wash and dry all the leaves and shred the plantain. Peel and grate the cucumber and crush the garlic. Slice the potato and mix everything together. Toss well with the vinaigrette.

Primrose

Spring

Primula vulgaris.
Primulaceae family.
Native perennial, common in woods,
hedgerows and grass.
Height: up to 8 inches/20 cm.
Flowers (yellow) March to May.

> Primrose, first-born child of Ver,
> Merry spring-time's harbinger.

Beaumont and Fletcher, *Two Noble Kinsmen*

This favourite of flowers gets its name from the Latin *prima rosa*, the first flower of the spring. Both the leaves and the flowers are edible although, personally, I would rather put them in a jar of water and enjoy looking at them: but for those without my aesthetic qualms, here are some ideas for eating them.

Primrose Salad

4 oz/100 g small spinach leaves
4 oz/100 g bean sprouts
10–12 young primrose leaves
vinaigrette
a few flowers

Shred the spinach leaves and mix with the bean sprouts and primrose leaves. Dress with vinaigrette and sprinkle the flowers over the top.

Primrose Leaves Cooked with Sorrel

2 cups primrose leaves, pressed down
2 cups sorrel leaves, pressed down
3 oz/75 g butter
flour

$\frac{1}{4}$ pint/150 ml top of the milk or cream
salt and pepper

Shred the leaves. Melt the butter and cook the primrose leaves in it until tender. Add the shredded sorrel and cook down until it turns brownish green. Sprinkle with flour. Cook, stirring, for 2 or 3 minutes, then gradually add the hot milk or cream. Stir until thick, season to taste and serve with meat, fish or poultry.

Primrose Pie

8 oz/250 g sweet crust pastry
1 lb/500 g cooking apples
4 oz/100 g caster sugar
a handful of primrose petals

Line a greased pie dish with half of the pastry, rolled out very thinly. Peel, core and slice the apples and shake them with some of the caster sugar until they are well coated. Place them in the pastry-lined dish. Put the petals and remaining sugar over the apples and cover with the rest of the pastry. Flute the edges together with a fork, brush with milk and bake at 350°F/180°C or gas mark 4 for 25 minutes or until golden brown. Serve with cream. For 4.

Other Uses for Primroses:

Primrose wine: make according to the instructions for flower wines on page 222.

Primrose vinegar: see vinegars on page 198.

Crystallized primroses: these make a beautiful garnish for cakes and mousses. For the method, see page 95.

Purslane (Common)

(*Green Purslane*)

Summer

Portulaca oleracea.
Portulacaceae family.
Found on sandy ground.
Height: up to 6 inches/15 cm.
Flowers (yellow) in July.

Purslane is becoming more commonly cultivated in this country and is still used in France as a constituent, with sorrel, of *soupe bonne femme*. It is rich in minerals and vitamins and makes an excellent salad vegetable.

To strew purslane around your bed used to be considered a protection from magic and a 'sure cure for blastings by lightning or planets and burning by gunpowder'!

Purslane with Eggs

> 1 bunch of purslane
> 2 oz/50 g butter
> 6 eggs
> salt and pepper

Strip the purslane leaves from their stalks and wash them well. Melt the butter and cook the purslane for 3 or 4 minutes until it has wilted. Beat the eggs and season them well. Pour them over the purslane and cook like an omelette, stirring a little until the eggs are cooked. Turn the mixture out on a flat dish and serve immediately. For 3.

Purslane Soup

> 1 bunch of purslane
> 3 oz/75 g butter
> 1 lb/500 g green peas
> 1 lettuce heart, shredded

a few sorrel leaves
2 onions, chopped
½ pint/300 ml milk and ½ pint/300 ml
    stock
salt and pepper

Strip the purslane leaves from their stalks and wash them. Melt the butter and cook all the vegetables in it until they are soft. Cover with the liquids, season and cook until tender. Liquidize and add more milk to thin out, if necessary. Check the seasoning and serve hot. For 4.

Lettuce and Purslane Salad

Here is a recipe from the seventeenth century, from none other than the Master Cook to King Charles II, a certain Giles Rose:

'Sallet of Lettice and Purslan.

Take of the newest Purslan, pick and wash it very well, swing it out, and lay it in the round of the Plate, and Lettice round about it, garnish the brims with Charvile and Flowers hashed together of divers colours, very small.'

Roses (Garden)

Summer

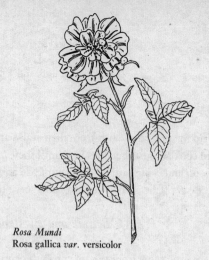

Rosa Mundi
Rosa gallica *var.* versicolor

Rosaceae family

The petals of cultivated and wild roses alike give a beautiful flavour to ice creams and jams, and are well worth using since the petals are just right for cooking at the point when the rose is over its peak. The more heavily scented the rose, the stronger the taste will be in the end result: the ideal rose to use is *Rosa gallica*, or the rose of Provins, known in the thirteenth century as 'The Apothecaries' Rose', as it retains its scent and flavour exceptionally well.

The white triangle at the base of the petal must be removed before using (this is called 'heeling').

Rose Water

Rinse some petals and cover with boiling water – you will be the best judge of how strong the flavour will be by the smell of the roses: add more petals to the quantity of water that you require if they are delicately scented. Cover and leave for 5 hours. Strain the rose water through a sieve, pressing the petals to squeeze out all the juice.

Crystallized Petals

These make a lovely and useful garnish for a meringue basket filled with whipped cream, and for mousses and ice creams of all kinds. For the method, see page 95.

Rose Ice Cream

½ cup dark-red rose petals
1½ tbsps caster sugar
¼ pint/150 ml rosé wine
¼ pint/150 ml double cream
1½ oz/40 g icing sugar
2 egg whites
12 crystallized rose petals (see page 95).

Wash the petals and shake them dry. Liquidize them for a minute with the caster sugar and the wine.

Beat the cream with the sifted icing sugar until it is thick. Stir in the rose mixture. Beat the egg whites until stiff, fold into the cream and put into an ice cream container. Cover and freeze. Serve garnished with crystallized rose petals.

Rose and Strawberry Ice

2 cups strawberries
4 oz/100 g sugar
1 tsp rose water (see page 162)
¾ pint/450 ml plain yoghurt
1 egg white

Purée the strawberries, sugar and rose water in the blender, then add to the yoghurt. Put into an ice tray and freeze; when mushy (after about 1 hour) fold in the very stiffly beaten egg white. Re-freeze and serve garnished with crystallized rose petals or mint sprigs.

Strawberry and Rose Dessert

3 eggs, separated
2 oz/50 g caster sugar
½ pint/300 ml milk
1 tsp vanilla essence
1 lb/500 g strawberries
a handful of dark-red rose petals
rose water (see page 162)
¼ pint/150 ml double cream

Beat the egg yolks with the sugar until they turn pale yellow and thick. Stir in the boiling milk and cook to a thick custard over hot water. Flavour with vanilla and chill.

Hull the strawberries and sprinkle them with caster sugar. Put in a glass bowl or into individual dishes. Liquidize the rose petals with a few drops of rose water, whip the cream and add the rose purée and the stiffly beaten egg whites. Fold into the custard and pile over the strawberries. Serve chilled. For 6.

Rose Petal Yoghurt

❦

the petals of 1 rose, washed and heeled
2 small cartons of plain yoghurt
sugar to taste

Liquidize all the ingredients and serve chilled or frozen: a lovely summer treat for children.

Rose Petal Tart

❦

1 sweet crust pastry flan case, baked
   blind (see page 224)
½ pint/300 ml double cream
2 egg yolks
2 tbsps caster sugar
1 family-size carton plain yoghurt
2–3 tbsps rose water (see page 162)
crystallized rose petals (see page 95)

Whip the cream until it is thick. Add the egg yolks, caster sugar and yoghurt and mix well. Add the rose water and pour into the pastry case. Bake at 325°F/170°C or gas mark 3 for 45 to 60 minutes until set. Cool and refrigerate. Sprinkle crystallized rose petals over the top just before serving.

Rose Pancakes

2 eggs
4 tbsps sugar
2 tbsps cornflour
½ pint/300 ml milk
4 tbsps chopped, heeled rose petals
1 tsp rose water (see page 162)

Beat the eggs with the sugar and, when they are thick and pale yellow, add the cornflour and mix in well. Pour on the boiling milk gradually, stirring until it is smooth. Over moderate heat, stir until the custard thickens, then add the finely chopped petals and rose water. Cool.

Combine:

1 lb/500 g cottage cheese
6 tbsps sultanas
2 tbsps rose honey (see below)
½ tsp grated lemon or lime peel
a dash of nutmeg or cinnamon

Add to the custard, refrigerate and use as a filling for cold sweet dessert pancakes (for batter, see page 225). Serves 6.

Rose Petal Honey

2 lb/1 kg liquid honey
1½ pints/1 litre rose water
juice of a lemon
pectin

Heat the honey gently, add the rose water and lemon juice and bring to the boil. Simmer for 10 minutes, then sprinkle a little pectin over the top. Boil 3 minutes longer. Strain, and boil hard until syrupy. Cool, stirring a little, then pot and seal.

Rose Petal Syrup

To serve with ice cream.

> 2 cups sugar
> 2 cups water
> 1 tbsp each orange and lemon juice
> 2 cups rose petals, wild or cultivated

Dissolve the sugar in the water and fruit juices over a low heat, then add the rose petals. Stir continuously for ½ to ¾ hour, keeping it just below simmering point. Cool a little, strain, pour into glass jars and store. This is particularly good with strawberry ice cream.

Rhubarb and Rose Petal Jam

> 1 lb/500g rhubarb
> 1 lb/500 g sugar
> juice of a lemon
> 2 handfuls rose petals

Cut the rhubarb into 1-inch/2.5 cm lengths and cover with the sugar and the lemon juice. Leave to stand overnight.

Chop the rose petals and add to the rhubarb. Cook to setting point, pot and seal.

Rose (Wild)

(*Dog Rose*)

Spring and autumn

Rosa canina.
Rosaceae family.
Native and common.
Height: up to 10 feet/3 m.
Flowers (pink and white) June to July.
Fruits (red) August to November.

Unkempt about those hedgerows blows
An unofficial English rose.

Rupert Brooke, 'Grantchester'

Rose Petal Salad

2 cups shredded petals, washed and heeled
6 spring onions, chopped
2 oz/50 g peanuts, chopped
½ oz/15 g sesame seeds
6 oz/175 g bean sprouts

Mix all the ingredients together and dress with a vinaigrette made with walnut oil. Serves 4.

Rose Petal Jelly

cooking apples
1 handful rose petals per 1 lb/500 g fruit
water
sugar

Chop and cook the apples in enough water to cover until they are soft.

Strain through a jelly bag overnight. To every 1 pint/600 ml liquid add
¾ lb/325 g sugar, dissolve over a low heat and then bring to the boil.

Heel the petals and add to the apple syrup. Boil together to setting
point, then strain, pot and seal.

Rose Petal Wine
❧

Wine can be made using rose petals (see Bibliography, Books Recommended for Wine-Making, page 238).

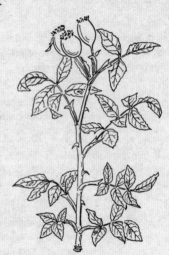

Rose Hips

'The fruit when it is ripe maketh
most pleasant meats and banqueting
dishes, as tarts and such like; the
making whereof I commit to the
cunning cook, and teeth to eate them
in the rich man's mouth' (Gerard).

Tea can also be made using rose
hips (see page 196). Crush them
slightly before infusing them.

Rose Hip and Apple Cheese
❧

2 lb/1 kg cooking apples
8 oz/250 g red rose hips
½ pint/300 ml fresh orange juice
¼ pint/150 ml water
sugar

Chop the apples. Slice the rose hips and tie them in a muslin bag. Put into
the pan with the orange juice and water and cook until the apples are soft.
Remove the rose hips. Sieve the apples and to every 1 lb/500 g pulp add
¾ lb/325 g sugar. Cook until thick, stirring all the time. Pot and seal. You
can use this cheese in the following recipe.

Rose Hip and Apple Snow

> 6 oz/175 g rose hip and apple cheese
>   (see above)
> 1 tbsp lemon juice
> 2 tbsps clear honey
> 3 tbsps rose hip syrup (see below)
> 2 egg whites

Reheat the cheese until it is soft, then add the lemon juice, honey and syrup. Beat the egg whites until they are very stiff and fold into the mixture. Pile into glasses, chill and serve sprinkled with chopped nuts. For 4.

Rose hip jelly and rose hip and apple jelly can be made in the same way as crab-apple jelly (see page 63).

Rose Hip Syrup

Well-known for its rich content of vitamin C, this is traditionally given to babies to make them the picture of health.

> 6 pints/3.5 litres water
> 3 lb/1.5 kg ripe rose hips
> 2 lb/1 kg sugar

Boil 4 pints/2.5 litres of the water. Slice the hips and put them into the water. Reheat to boiling point and skim while cooking for a few minutes. Cook for ½ hour. Strain through a jelly bag, then boil the remaining pulp with the rest of the water. Cool for ½ hour and strain as before.

Combine the two liquids and boil until reduced to about 3 pints/1.5 litres. Add the sugar and bring to the boil. Cook to a syrup, then cool. Pot and seal, and store in a dark cupboard.

Rose Hip Wine

A good country wine can be made from rose hips (see Bibliography, Books Recommended for Wine-Making, page 238).

Rowan

(*Mountain Ash*)

Autumn

Sorbus aucuparia.
Rosaceae family.
Native, common and found in woods, on
roadsides and in the mountains.
Height: up to 20 feet/15 m.
Fruits (orange) August to September.

In pre-Christian religions this tree was believed to offer protection against evil, and it was said that witches were powerless to harm anyone sheltering beneath it. The beautiful clusters of orange berries make a delicious jelly that goes very well with roast meats, hot or cold.

Rowan Berry Jelly

Following the instructions for making crab-apple jelly (see page 63), add 2 tablespoons lemon juice to every 4 lb/2 kg rowan berries.

For *rowan and crab-apple jelly*, use equal weights of fruit. For *rowan and apple jelly*, use equal weights of fruit. For *spiced rowan jelly*, add cloves and allspice berries, tied in a muslin bag, when cooking rowan and apple jelly. Make all these jellies following the method for crab-apple jelly on page 63, using 2 tablespoons lemon juice to every 4 lb/2 kg berries.

Rowan Berry Wine

Wine can also be made from rowan berries, following the method on page 221, allowing 4 days for pulp fermentation (see note 3).

Salad Burnet (PLATE VI)

Summer

Poterium sanguisorba.
Rosaceae family.
Native perennial, common in the
Midlands, particularly on chalky ground.
Height: up to 12 inches/30 cm.
Flowers (yellow-green) May to August.

This pretty herb with its fresh green serrated leaves grows abundantly in grass on chalk. With its cucumber flavour it makes a refreshing addition to green salads and also a lovely summer soup. The leaves can be used to make tea (see page 196).

It was grown and used as a salad herb in the sixteenth century, and was among the plants taken by the Pilgrim Fathers to the New World, where it has become naturalized in the wild.

Iced Salad Burnet Soup

1 large bunch salad burnet
2 oz/50 g butter
1 oz/25 g rice
¾ pint/450 ml good stock
salt and pepper
cream

Strip the salad burnet leaves from their stalks, wash and dry them. Melt the butter and cook the leaves in it until they have wilted and have absorbed most of the butter. Add the rice and stir, then add the stock, stirring all the time. Bring to the boil and then simmer until the rice is cooked. Liquidize and season to taste. Add a little cream and chill. Serves 4.

Salad Burnet and Cream Cheese Mould

1 large bunch salad burnet
1 oz/25 g butter
6 oz/175 g cream cheese
1 tsp grated onion
salt and pepper
½ oz/15 g gelatine
¼ pint/150 ml stock
2 tbsps vinegar
1 tbsp caster sugar
pinch of mace and of powdered
   coriander
¼ pint/150 ml double cream

Oil a ring mould (1 pint or 600 ml). Strip the leaves from the stalks of the salad burnet and chop them very finely. Cook them gently in the melted butter. Mash the cream cheese with the onion and seasonings. Soak the gelatine in a little warm water until dissolved, then add the cheese, the stock and the burnet with the vinegar, sugar and spices. Fold in the whipped cream. Pour into the mould to set. Turn out the next day. Serves 4.

Garnish with watercress and slivers of green pepper.

Samphire

Summer

(a) Marsh Samphire or Glasswort (PLATE VI)
Salicornia europaea.
Chenopodiaceae family.
A native annual succulent, found on mud
flats around the coast.
Height: up to 10 inches/20 cm.
Flowers (orange) in August and
September.

(b) Rock Samphire (PLATE VI)
Crithmum maritimum.
Umbelliferae family.
Native perennial, common on the south
coast, in Wales and southern Ireland.
Found on rocks, cliffs and shingle.
Height: up to 22 inches/30 cm.
Flowers (yellow) June to August.

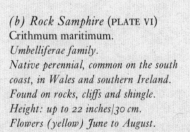

> The crows and choughs that wing the midway air
> Show scarce so gross as beetles; halfway down
> Hangs one that gathers samphire, dreadful trade!
> Methinks he seems no bigger than his head.
> The fishermen that walk upon the beach
> Appear like mice . . .

William Shakespeare, *King Lear*

There are two kinds of samphire, rock and marsh, and it is the former to which Shakespeare alludes in *King Lear*. Collecting either kind can be a hazardous occupation, so watch your step on the cliffs and rocks or the slippery mud flats. Gathering samphire, however, is not as sinister as Shakespeare makes it sound, and picking marsh samphire is in fact nothing less than a wonderful opportunity to get yourself and everything you subsequently touch completely covered in old-fashioned mud. It makes an expedition with its own unique character: slimy mud flats by the sea on summer days, deserted by the saner members of civilization, just the company of a few distant boats in the creek. It requires caution, however. Don't go alone, and keep an eye on the tide which may be coming in fast – and stay close to children because the mud is deceptive and can be dangerously deep.

Armed with large plastic bags, you can collect great quantities at a time – samphire grows prolifically and is easily picked since the mud is so soft. You must go at low tide, equipped with wellington boots and your very oldest clothes, and when you get the samphire home you will have to give it – and yourself probably – several washes in cold water, preferably at an outside tap, to free it completely of all the mud. Your efforts will be well rewarded by the astonishingly good taste and texture of this sea-asparagus.

Boiled Marsh Samphire

Cook the well-washed samphire, roots and all, in unsalted boiling water for 10 minutes. Serve immediately on a hot platter, as samphire loses its heat very rapidly.

Holding it by the root, dip the green part into melted butter and pull the succulent covering off its inner fibrous skeleton with your teeth.

With any leftovers of cold cooked samphire, strip the green part off the stem and pile it on to fresh buttered bread: it is a delicious way of eating it.

Alternatively, serve it cold with mayonnaise, or hot with *beurre noir* (see page 225).

Samphire and Mushroom Salad

Marsh samphire and wild mushrooms (see page 136) are in season at the same time and their contrasting textures make a delicious salad.

Use the young, tender, single shoots of samphire for this: they are about 6 inches/15 cm high and can be used in any salad, green or mixed, because their inner fibrous stem has not yet become tough. Wash them well and cut the fibrous parts into 1-inch/2.5-cm lengths. Slice the mushrooms and mix with the samphire. Dress with a garlic vinaigrette and leave to marinate for a couple of hours before serving as an hors d'œuvre.

Marsh Samphire Sauce

4 oz/100 g young marsh samphire
  shoots
1 pint/600 ml stock
2 tbsps wine vinegar
4 diced gherkins
capers
juice and peel of a lemon
½ pint/300 ml hollandaise sauce
pepper and nutmeg

Wash and chop the samphire and simmer it in the stock with the vinegar for 30 minutes. Drain and add to the gherkins, capers, lemon juice and rind. Stir into the hollandaise and season to taste.

This sauce was traditionally served with slices of meat placed on fried bread and garnished with fresh samphire and barberries.

Pickled Marsh Samphire

This is a welcome and tasty addition to the larder: samphire pickles well (better than it freezes – it can be frozen, but it loses a certain something in the process) yet, preserved in vinegar, it retains its unique sea-flavour. It is delicious with bread and cheese.

Pick the young shoots of samphire that grow as a single stem about 6 to 8 inches/15 to 20 cm high. Chop the tender parts of the stems and cut into 1-inch/2.5-cm lengths. Put into screw-top jars and cover with cold spiced vinegar (see page 28). Seal well and store for 2 months before using. Gerard's comment: 'The leaves kept in pickle, and eaten in sallads with oile and vinegar, is a pleasant sauce for meat.'

To Cook Rock Samphire
✸

Wash the plant well and remove slimy leaves or tough stalks. Boil for 15 minutes and serve with melted butter; eat, as marsh samphire, dipped in melted butter, eating the fleshy green parts of the leaves pulled off the inner fibrous network. Left until cold, the leaves are delicious with bread and butter.

Rock Samphire Pickle
✸

> rock samphire
> brine (6 oz/175 g salt to 1 quart/1 litre
>   water)
> white wine vinegar

Soak the young leaves in the brine for 3 or 4 hours. Put in a pan with 3 parts vinegar to 1 part brine, enough to cover the samphire. Cover with a lid and heat for 30 minutes. Remove from the heat and leave to stand, covered, until cold. Pack into airtight jars and cover with the liquid. Add more plain vinegar, if needed, to cover the leaves.

Seabeet

Summer

Beta vulgaris, *ssp*. maritima.
Chenopodiaceae family.
Native annual, biennial or perennial.
Common on salt marshes and shores
except in Scotland.
Height: up to 3 feet/1 m.
Flowers (green) June to September.

This is the wild version of cultivated beet and its thick shiny spinach-like leaves are rich in vitamins A and C. Cook it exactly as you would spinach: it makes a very good base for *œufs florentines*.

Seakale

Summer

Crambe maritima.
Cruciferae family.
Native perennial, found on sandy shores
and rocks, often on the tide line, on south-
east coasts only.
Height: up to 20 inches/50 cm.
Flowers (white) May to August.

The young stems of this increasingly rare plant can be boiled for 15 to 20 minutes in salted water and eaten like asparagus with melted butter or hollandaise sauce. Perhaps, however, this beautiful plant with its blue-grey leaves is best left alone for a while and given a chance to re-establish itself in the wild.

Sea Purslane

Summer

Halimione portulacoides.
Chenopodiaceae family.
Native of salt marshes, common on the
English and Welsh coastlines.
Height: up to 30 inches/80 cm.
Flowers (yellow-brown) July to
September.

The succulent leaves of this little shrub are good in salads when they are
young, and can also be boiled and served with butter or cream like French
beans – the addition of a little garlic makes them even more appetizing.
The leaves can also be preserved, like samphire, in spiced vinegar (see page
28) and make a welcome variation in the standard range of pickles.

Seaweeds

Many seaweeds have been eaten for generations and were highly valued for their richness of vitamins and minerals, particularly iodine. They grow abundantly and are quick and easy to gather.

(a) Laver (PLATE VI)

Summer

Porphyra umbilicalis.
Rhodophyllaceae family.

This seaweed, which clings to rocks like wet brown silk, is found on all shores, in rock pools, around Britain but it is particularly common in Wales and the West of England. It is one of our oldest saladings and it grows over stones and rocks, especially those covered with sand. Its translucent purplish-brown leaf is sold in shops in the West Country and Wales but it is certainly worth the easy task of gathering it oneself in April and May. It has high iodine and gelatine contents and is rich in mineral salts. The Chinese and Japanese cultivate it and it plays an important role in Oriental cookery.

Laverbread

Laverbread is the traditional name for laver purée.

Wash the laver well and cook it in a double saucepan over boiling water until it is tender. It dissolves into a purée and will keep in airtight jars for several days.

The customary way of using laverbread in Wales is to roll it in oatmeal and fry it in hot bacon fat to serve for breakfast. (This tasty morsel would make an original addition to a mixed grill: alternatively, combine laverbread with oatmeal and fry as you would a potato cake, until golden on both sides.)

Laver Sauce

> 2 cups laverbread
> 2 oz/50 g butter
> juice of ½ lemon or ½ Seville orange

Heat the purée in the melted butter, add the lemon or orange juice and serve with mutton or lamb.

Creamed Laver

Add some laverbread to a generous quantity of béchamel sauce (see page 224), and serve, well-heated, as a side vegetable.

Laver Salad

The prepared laverbread is excellent eaten as a salad dressed with a strong vinaigrette.

(b) Carragheen (Irish Moss)

Summer

Chondrus crispus.
Gigartinaceae family.

The purplish-brown fan-shaped fronds of this seaweed are to be found along the Atlantic seaboard, growing over rocks and stones. It is a vegetable gelatine and used medicinally as an emollient. It is at its best when picked in the late spring and early summer and is traditionally used to make custards and blancmanges.

Irish Moss Custard

> 1 cup fresh moss, soaked in water until
>   it uncurls (a few minutes)
> 2 cups milk
> 1 egg yolk, beaten in ½ cup cold milk
> sugar
> vanilla or ginger
> 1 egg white, stiffly beaten

Simmer the moss in the milk until it disintegrates. Press through a sieve. Beat in the egg yolk and milk mixture, then stir over a very low heat until thick. Sweeten and flavour to taste. Fold in the egg white and serve, chilled, in glasses. For 4.

Irish Moss Blancmange

> 3 cups milk
> 1 cup fresh moss, soaked in water until
>   it uncurls (a few minutes)
> sugar and flavouring (vanilla or ginger)

Simmer the moss in the milk until it disintegrates. Sieve, sweeten and flavour to taste. Pour into a bowl to set. Turn out when cold and stiff.

To Dry Carragheen

Wash and soak the fronds until they are bleached and creamy-white. Trim off the tough stalks, dry until brittle in the sun or in a slow oven, then store in bags in a dry place.

Shepherd's Purse

Summer

Capsella bursa-pastoris.
Cruciferae family.
Common and widespread. Annual.
Height: up to 12 inches/30 cm.
Flowers (white) all the year.

This well-known little weed is widely eaten in China and is commonly to be found on the markets there. It tastes like a spicy variety of cabbage and is well worth adding to salads, or cooking in the same ways as chickweed (see page 41).

Sloe (PLATE VI)

Autumn

Prunus spinosa.
Rosaceae family.
Native, common in hedges and scrub
except in northern Scotland.
Height: up to 14 feet/4 m.
Fruits (bluish-black) from September to
November.

Many haws, many sloes,
Many cold toes.

Popular saying

Sloes are best gathered after the first frost and, although very bitter to eat straight from the tree, they make a lovely jelly. And as for sloe gin – there is something about it that makes Christmas Christmas. Its wonderful dark pink colour and its thick sweet warmth are an integral part of the festivities, and later on, in the bleak winter months, it is a welcome companion on long dark evenings.

Sloe Gin

To every ½ lb/250 g sloes allow ¾ pint/450 ml gin, 2 oz/50 g sugar and 6 blanched almonds, bruised but unpeeled.

Wash, dry and prick the sloes with a darning needle. Put them into bottles with the sugar and the almonds and cover with the gin. Shake every few days to dissolve the sugar. Store for at least 3 months – but it tastes much better if you are strong-minded enough to leave it for a year.

Sloe Jelly

✥

sloes
water
sugar

Wash the sloes and prick each one with a darning needle. Put into a pan with a little water – just enough to cover – and simmer until soft (about an hour). Strain through a jelly bag overnight. To every pint/600 ml liquid add 1 lb/500 g sugar. Dissolve over a low heat, bring to the boil and cook to setting point. Pot and seal.

Variations: For *sloe and apple jelly*, use equal quantities of fruit. For *sloe and blackberry jelly*, use 4 lb/2 kg blackberries to every 1 lb/500 g sloes. For *sloe cheese*, make as for bullace cheese on page 29.

Sloe Wine

✥

Here is a recipe from Dorothy Wise's *Home Made Country Wines* (Hamlyn, 1971).

'1 quart sloes
1 quart boiling water
1 lb loaf sugar

'*Method:* Add boiling water to each quart of sloes. Stand 4 days, stirring once or twice each day. Strain and add to each quart of liquid 1 lb loaf sugar. Stand another 4 days, stirring each day. Bottle after it has well settled. Do not cork tightly until finished working.

'Mrs F.J. Morris, Newtown, Mont.'

Snowberry

Autumn

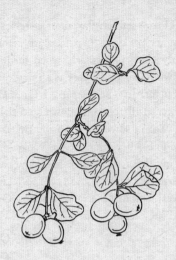

Symphoricarpos rivularis.
Caprifoliaceae family.
Introduced shrub, common in the wild.
Height: up to 10 feet/3 m.
Fruits (white) September to November.

The crunchy berries of this pretty shrub are edible but rather tasteless – they are best used as an addition to fruit crumbles and pies for their appetizing texture.

Sorrel (Common) (PLATE VII)

(*see also* Wood Sorrel on page 216)

Summer

Rumex acetosa.
Polygonaceae family.
Native perennial, common on roadsides
and in fields and woods.
Height: up to 3 feet/1 m.
Flowers May to June.

The lovely lemony flavour of sorrel leaves makes a distinctive difference to summer cooking; their uses are manifold – they are good eaten raw in sandwiches, particularly when made with beef dripping, and are well known to weary walkers as a thirst quencher, simply chewed straight off the plant. In *The Shepherd's Calendar*, John Clare says of sorrel: 'The mower gladly chews it down, and slakes his thirst the best he may.'

Put some sorrel leaves inside a mackerel, with a knob of butter, and bake it in foil. They are delicious cooked in butter and put in omelettes – try mixing them with chives and cow parsley. The leaves make marvellous fritters (see page 53). As a cooked vegetable, sorrel goes very well with fish or veal, and makes excellent soups. Of course it is familiar to many in its cultivated form.

Sorrel and Garlic Soup

> 1 handful sorrel leaves
> 4 oz/100 g butter
> 4 cloves garlic
> 1½ oz/40 g flour
> 1 pint/600 ml chicken stock
> salt and pepper
> cream

Wash and chop the sorrel leaves. Melt half the butter over a low heat and add the whole, peeled garlic cloves. Cook for a minute or so, then add the sorrel. Cook slowly for about 10 minutes.

In a thick pan melt the rest of the butter, add the flour and then gradually stir in the heated stock. Bring to the boil and simmer for about 10 minutes.

Add the sorrel and garlic, mix well and liquidize. Season to taste and finish with the cream. Serves 4.

Sorrel and Tomato Soup

> 1½ lb/750 g skinned tomatoes
> 1 oz/25 g butter
> 1 handful sorrel leaves, washed and
>   chopped

garlic (optional)
salt and pepper
1½ pints/1 litre chicken stock
cream

Chop the tomatoes finely and cook in the melted butter until softened. Add the sorrel and optional garlic and cook for a few minutes until the leaves have wilted and darkened, then season to taste. Stir in the stock gradually and heat through. Finish with the cream. Serves 4.

Sorrel Purée

Wash and chop sorrel leaves and cook for about 10 minutes in melted butter. Add some béchamel sauce (see page 224) and a little cream if desired. Mix thoroughly, season to taste and serve as a garnish for veal or fish, or chilled with cold poached mackerel fillets. It is exceptionally good served with fried kidneys.

Sorrel Chiffonnade

Wash the sorrel leaves and shred them finely. Melt a generous amount of butter and cook the sorrel leaves until the liquid has evaporated. Add some cream and heat through.

This can be preserved in jars if pressed down well, sealed with clarified butter (see page 225) and kept in the refrigerator.

Braised Sorrel

1 lb/500 g sorrel leaves
½ pint/300 ml water
salt
½ pint/300 ml béchamel sauce made
 with stock (see page 224)

Cook the leaves in the boiling salted water and simmer until the volume is greatly reduced. Drain and add to the béchamel sauce. Put in a baking dish and cook at 325°F/170°C or gas mark 3 for 1 hour.

Sorrel Sauce for Pork

2 slices wholemeal bread
1 cooking apple
1 tbsp vinegar
a little sugar
salt and pepper
1 small bunch sorrel leaves
water or stock
marigold petals

Soak the bread in water. Peel, core and chop the apple. Cook the bread and apple together with the vinegar and sugar in a little water until well amalgamated. Season. Add the finely chopped sorrel and cook for 5 minutes, stirring well. Thin out with stock and serve sprinkled with marigold petals.

Sorrel and Mushroom Soufflé

2 shallots
3 oz/75 g butter
8 oz/250 g mushrooms
seasoning
1 handful sorrel leaves
1 oz/25 g flour
½ pint/300 ml milk
4 eggs, separated

Chop the shallots finely and soften in 1 oz/25 g of butter over a gentle heat. Wash and chop the mushrooms and add to the pan. Cover and cook very gently, turning occasionally, until the mushrooms are soft. Season to taste and add the washed, chopped sorrel leaves. Cook for a further 5 minutes.

In a different pan melt the rest of the butter, add the flour and gradually stir in the boiling milk. Season well. Off the heat add the egg yolks, mixing thoroughly. Add the mushroom and sorrel mixture.

Beat the egg whites with a pinch of salt until they are very stiff. Fold into the base and put into a greased soufflé dish. Cook at 400°F/200°C or gas mark 6 for 2 minutes and then turn the heat down to 375°F/190°C or gas mark 5 and cook for a further 20 to 25 minutes.

Sorrel Quiche

> 1 bunch sorrel leaves
> 1 oz/25 g butter
> salt and pepper
> 1 small carton double cream
> 2 eggs
> an 8-inch/20-cm pastry case, baked
>   blind (see page 224)

Wash and chop the sorrel leaves and wilt them in the melted butter over a low heat until soft and brownish. Season with salt and add a little cream.

Beat the eggs and season them, then add the rest of the cream. Add to the sorrel, pour into the pastry case and cook at 400°F/200°C or gas mark 6 for 10 minutes, then turn the heat down to 350°F/180°C or gas mark 4 and cook for 20 minutes longer. Serve warm or cold.

Variations: for *sorrel and walnut quiche*, add 2 oz/50 g chopped walnut meats to the sorrel and egg mixture. For *sorrel and garlic quiche*, add 2 cloves of crushed garlic to the sorrel while it is cooking in the butter.

All these quiches are good cooked in individual pastry cases as tartlets.

Sow Thistle (Common or Smooth) <small>(PLATE VII)</small>

Summer

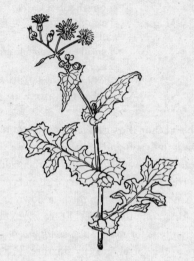

Sonchus oleraceus.
Compositae family.
Native annual, common except in
Scotland.
Height: up to 5 feet/1.5 m.
Flowers (yellow) June to August.

Theseus is said to have dined off a dish of sow thistles before conquering the Minotaur. They have been well known as a popular vegetable for centuries, and not without cause. Sow thistle leaves have a taste all their own and many a guest at my table has been surprised by their excellence. They are one of the very best of the hedgerow greens, and are delicious mixed with dandelions and nettles, cooked and tossed in butter and served hot. It sounds unlikely, but the first time I tried sow thistle it was a balmy summer day when the idea of shopping seemed tedious and it was far easier to go out for a walk and collect some leaves. I did so, and had a delicious meal: luckily there were no minotaurs around that day.

To Cook Sow Thistle as a Vegetable

Wash the tender young leaves and cook them in a little water, with a knob of butter, over a low heat, stirring constantly. Season and add some chopped chives or spring onions. Cook until soft.

Sow Thistle and Wild Herb Soup

    3 tbsps butter
    1 cup chopped shallots or chives
    2 cups chopped sow thistle, garlic
        mustard, yarrow, rocket, plantain,
        etc., pressed down
    3 cups hot water
    $\frac{1}{3}$ cup rice
    salt
    2–3 cups milk

Melt the butter and cook the shallots or chives until they are soft. Stir half the chopped greens into the butter and cook for a minute or two, until they are wilted. Add the water gradually and bring to the boil, then stir in the rice and the salt. Cook for 20 minutes and then liquidize. Thin out with milk and season carefully. In another pan, cook the other half of the chopped greens gently in a tablespoon of butter for several minutes. Add a little cream and mix with the soup base. Reheat and serve. For 6.

Sweet Cicely

Summer

Myrrhis odorata.
Umbelliferae family.
*Perennial, common in northern England
and West Scotland in hedgerows and
grassland.*
Height: up to 3 feet/1 m.
Flowers (cream) April to June.

A sprig of this delicate-looking herb, with its lacy leaves, added to the cooking of fruit or jams cuts down the quantity of sugar required by as much as half. Added to the cooking of sorrel or dandelion leaves, sweet cicely takes the edge off their slight bitterness.

Tansy (PLATE VII)

Summer

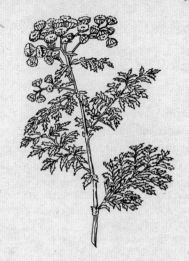

Tanacetum vulgare.
Compositae family.
Native perennial of hedgerows, verges
and waste places. Fairly common except
in Ireland.
Height: up to 3 feet/1 m.
Flowers (yellow) July to September.

This beautiful old-fashioned herb used to be one of those most commonly grown in herb gardens and was much used medicinally. Its thick fern-like leaves, and yellow flowers which look like smooth, round buttons, are as enticing to look at as the leaves are to taste. Tansy has a bad reputation for having a bitter flavour because it was originally used in Easter-time recipes as a penance in remembrance of the bitter herbs eaten at the Feast of the Passover. Indeed, it is not to everyone's taste: the Rev. C.A. Johns in *Flowers of the Field* (1884) says it 'forms the principal ingredient in the nauseous dish called *Tansy Pudding*'. But not for nothing was it so widely grown in old English gardens – to me the taste is spicy and quite incomparable. I have found it to be delicious in salads as well as highly recommendable in the recipes below.

The tansy cakes are spicy and tasty. One summer afternoon my young daughter and her friends demolished a plateful of them, and that has to be the ultimate seal of approval. They were traditionally eaten at Trinity College, Cambridge, on Easter Monday and Tuesday.

Tansy Cakes

4 oz/100 g flour
a pinch of salt
2 oz/50 g butter

2 oz/50 g sugar
1 tsp baking powder
1 tsp chopped tansy leaves
1 egg
milk

Sift the flour with the salt. Rub in the butter, add the sugar and baking powder and mix in the chopped tansy. Beat the egg well and add it to the mixture with a little milk to make a good dough.

Grease individual bun tins, put 1 tablespoon of the mixture into each one and bake at 450°F/230°C or gas mark 8 for 12 to 15 minutes. Serve warm with butter.

Tansy

5 eggs
2 egg whites
½ pint/300 ml cream
nutmeg
1 tbsp biscuit crumbs
a sprig or two of tansy
sugar to taste
1 orange and 1 lemon

Beat the eggs and egg whites well and pour on the cream. Season with nutmeg and add the biscuit crumbs and the chopped tansy. Add sugar to taste.

Pour into a buttered fireproof dish and cook at 325°F/170°C or gas mark 3 for 30 minutes or until set. Turn out on a plate, sprinkle with sugar and freshly pressed orange juice. Garnish with slices of orange and lemon. It is good either hot or cold.

Tansy Pudding

2 oz/50 g ground almonds
1½ oz/40 g butter
2 oz/50 g biscuit crumbs
a sprig of tansy

a pinch of nutmeg
2 tbsps golden syrup
a small glass of brandy
3 or 4 eggs
½ pint/300 ml milk
¼ pint/150 ml double cream
some slices of lemon peel

Rub the ground almonds into the butter and crumble the biscuit crumbs in lightly with the chopped tansy and nutmeg. Add the warmed syrup and the brandy. Put in an ovenproof dish.

Beat the eggs with the milk, pour carefully over the mixture, and bake at 325°F/170°C or gas mark 3 for about 45 minutes or until set. Serve cold, decorated with whipped cream and garnished with the slices of lemon peel.

'Minnow Tansies

'The minnows are washed well in salt, and their heads and tails cut off, and their guts taken out, and not washed after, they prove excellent for that use that is being fried with yolks of eggs, the flowers of cowslips and of primroses and a little tansy; thus they make a dainty shell of meat.'

Izaak Walton, *The Compleat Angler*

Teas and Tisanes

Infusions made from fresh or dried leaves of wild plants, flowers and herbs can have both tonic and cosmetic values. When using fresh leaves or petals, use 3 teaspoonfuls (chopped) per cup; use half the amount if they are dried, as the flavour is that much more concentrated. Bruise the fresh leaves before pouring boiling water over them, and leave the infusion to stand for 7 to 10 minutes. Then strain and sweeten with honey if desired. A tisane is, strictly speaking, the name given to a herb tea only. You can try adding herbs or leaves or flowers to China tea to vary the flavour.

To dry leaves, strip them off their stalks and lay them on newspaper in a warm dry place (an airing cupboard is ideal) for 2 or 3 days, turning them occasionally, until they are brittle. Store in airtight jars.

Such teas and tisanes can be made from the following: angelica leaves, bilberry leaves, blackberry leaves, borage leaves, chamomile flowers, comfrey leaves, cowslip leaves, dandelion leaves, elder leaves, hop leaves, juniper berries, lady's mantle leaves, lime flowers, marigold flowers, marjoram leaves, meadowsweet flowers and leaves, mint, nettle leaves, pine needles, rose hips, salad burnet leaves, thyme leaves, violet leaves and yarrow leaves.

Thyme

Summer

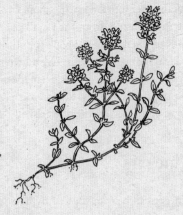

Thymus praecox.
Labiatae family.
Tiny native shrub of dry grassy uplands,
common in the north and west.
Height: up to 3 inches/7 cm.
Flowers (purplish-red) May to August.

This pretty herb is proverbially a favourite with the fairies and it is also much loved by bees. The flavour of wild thyme is milder than that of the cultivated variety so it can be used lavishly. Pick it while it is in full bloom to get the best flavour.

Put sprigs of thyme over roasting meat, or inside a chicken while it cooks. It is good for flavouring meat balls and stuffings, and goes particularly well with mushrooms and courgettes as a garnish. A tea can be made from the leaves (see page 196) which is said to be good for colds, catarrh and sore throats, and is also soporific.

Thyme Jelly

Add a generous number of thyme sprigs to crab-apple jelly (see page 63) or to an apple jelly made with the same method. Serve with cold meats and poultry.

Liver with Thyme

¾ lb/325 g lamb's liver
salt and pepper
thyme and garlic
6 oz/175 g streaky bacon
olive oil

Cut the liver into long strips about ½ inch/1 cm thick and season well. Strip the thyme leaves from their stalks and chop. Crush the garlic. Take the rinds off the bacon and cook it until it is very crisp.

Heat the oil gently and cook the thyme and garlic in it for a few minutes. Then turn up the heat and, when the oil is very hot, toss the liver in the pan and cook very rapidly so that it is crisp on the outside and pink inside. Serve immediately with the crisped bacon, buttered rice and a side salad.

Vinegars

Vinegar can be transformed by having steeped in it any of the following berries, flowers or roots until they have imparted their flavour: blackberries, elderberries, elderflowers, horseradish, mint, primroses, violets and nasturtium flowers. Allow a week or two, changing the flowers or berries from time to time when they look tired. Add chopped shallots if you wish. The amount of herb to vinegar depends on the strength of flavour you require. Use white wine vinegar.

Violet (Sweet)

Spring

Viola odorata.
Violaceae family.
Native perennial, common except in the
north and in Ireland. Found in hedgerows
and on the edges of woods.
Height: up to 3 inches/8 cm.
Flowers (purple or white) February to
April.

The scented violet is a plant of great beauty; it differs from many of its close relatives, like the dog violet, in that these have virtually no smell. Its name is associated with modesty; and, for the Greeks, *Viola odorata* was the flower of Aphrodite – indeed it has been used in perfumes and love potions throughout history. The designer of the Unicorn Tapestries placed violets around the hooves of the captured unicorn, and folklore has it that to dream of violets means good luck ahead. It has been renowned for its culinary virtues for centuries and is a famous flavouring in confectionery.

Like the cowslip, however, this flower is suffering from overpicking: so treat it with respect when you find it in the wild. The answer is to grow it yourself if you want to use it in cooking. It is possible to obtain seeds of *Viola odorata* through good seed catalogues. So let the violet grow where it will in the wild, and not suffer the same fate as the cowslip.

A Fourteenth-Century Violet Sweet

'Take flowers of violet and boil them, press them, break them small, temper them up with almonds milk or good cows milk and boil it with almond flour or flour of rice. Sugar it enough and put cream thereto, and colour it, with the same that flowers be on above.'

Violet Sweet (Twentieth-Century Version)

a small bunch of fresh violets
½ pint/300 ml milk
4 tbsps ground rice
a few chopped almonds and 4 tsps
    ground almonds
2 oz/50 g sugar
1 large carton double cream
crystallized violets

Infuse the violets in the hot milk for 5 minutes, then strain it over the ground rice, the almonds and sugar. Heat gently until it thickens. Add half of the whipped cream and chill. Decorate with whipped cream and crystallized violets. Serves 4.

Violets are at their most useful crystallized or candied (see pages 95 and 94). They make a beautiful garnish and are delicious in a soufflé.

Violet Soufflé

2 oz/50 g butter
2 tbsps flour
½ pint/300 ml hot milk
2 oz/50 g sugar
1 tbsp kümmel
4 eggs, separated
½ cup candied violets

Melt the butter and stir in the flour. Add the hot milk gradually, stirring all the time until the mixture is smooth. Cool, and add the sugar and the kümmel. Beat in the egg yolks one by one. Beat the egg whites until they are stiff and fold in. Add the candied violets and pour into a greased and sugared soufflé dish. Put a wreath of candied violets on top and cook at 375°F/190°C or gas mark 5 for 20 minutes and serve immediately. For 4.

Violet Ice Cream (1)

1 small carton double cream
1 small carton single cream
3 oz/75 g caster sugar
2 oz/50 g brown breadcrumbs
1 oz/25 g sugar crystals or crushed
   barley sugar
1 egg white
crystallized violets

Whip the creams with the sugar until stiff, then fold in the breadcrumbs, sugar crystals and the stiffly beaten egg white. Cover and freeze. Sprinkle lavishly with crystallized violets before serving.

Violet Ice Cream (2)

a bunch of violets
1 large carton double cream
3 oz/75 g icing sugar
violet colouring

2 egg whites
crystallized violets

Strip the petals from the violets and infuse them in the hot cream. Leave until cold. Then whip it with the sieved sugar until stiff and add a drop or two of colouring. Whip the egg whites until stiff and fold into the cream. Put into a container, cover and freeze. Serve decorated with crystallized petals. For 6.

Violet Jam

½ lb/250 g violet flowers
1 pint/600 ml boiling water
1½ lb/750 g sugar

Put three quarters of the flowers into a bowl and pour over them the boiling water. Cover and leave for 15 hours. Strain the liquid, add the sugar and stir over a low heat until dissolved. Bring to the boil, add the remaining flowers and cook to setting point. Pour into small jars and cover.

Violet Paste

Pound violet petals in a mortar with a little lemon juice. Add twice their weight in sifted sugar and put in a pan over a low heat. Stir the mixture gently until the sugar has dissolved but do not boil it. Put on to a plate to dry out completely, then store in a box between layers of greaseproof paper.

Violet Liqueur

Make in the same way as carnation liqueur (see page 97).

Violet Leaves

These used to be eaten in various ways; they are a tasty addition to salads and also make very good sweet fritters (see page 53), served sprinkled with caster sugar. The leaves can also be made into a chiffonnade as for sorrel (see page 187), or cooked as any other green – they are said to be good for the kidneys. Both tea (see page 196) and vinegar (see page 198) can be made using violets.

Violet Salad (1)

1 lb/500 g young spinach leaves mixed with violet leaves
6 oz/175 g mushrooms
1 tsp lemon juice
1 tsp garlic olive oil
salt, pepper and thyme
2 oz/50 g water chestnuts
2 hard-boiled eggs
soy sauce
1 cup violet flowers
1 oz/25 g croûtons

Wash and shred the spinach leaves and the violet leaves and slice the mushrooms. Marinate all together in the lemon juice, garlic oil and seasonings for several hours.

Just before serving, add the sliced water chestnuts and quartered eggs, season and dress with the soy sauce. Toss in the violet flowers and serve immediately, garnished with the croûtons. For 6.

Violet Salad (2)

Make a salad of chopped chicory, celery and violet leaves, dress it with vinaigrette and garnish with violets.

Wall Lettuce

Summer

Mycelis muralis.
Compositae family.
Native perennial, found on walls and
rocks. Common in England and Wales.
Height: up to 3 feet/1 m.
Flowers (yellow) July to September.

The leaves can be used in salads in all the same ways as dandelion leaves.

Walnut

Summer and autumn

Juglans regia.
Juglandaceae family.
Height: up to 100 feet/30 m.
Fruits September to October.

The walnut rightly merits its gastronomic reputation. However, as in the case of mushrooms, there are already a great number of cookbooks containing a wide range of recipes for walnuts. So suffice it to say here that walnuts are delicious in ice creams, in stuffings, in cookies, in salads and sauces and, chopped, in sandwiches. They make a distinctive difference to an *aïllade toulousaine* or, as a garnish, to vichyssoise. I have restricted myself here to ways of preserving walnuts – except for the first four recipes which are such old favourites that they had to be included.

Walnut Soup

1 oz/25 g butter
1 medium onion
2 sticks celery
4 oz/100 g shelled walnuts
1½ pints/1 litre stock
a small carton of cream

Melt the butter; chop the onion and celery very finely and cook gently until soft. Liquidize the walnuts in a little of the stock and mix into the vegetables. Cook gently and add more stock gradually; season to taste and finish with the cream. Serves 4.

Walnut Tart

The English equivalent of – and worthy competitor to – America's Pecan Pie.

For the pie crust:
8 oz/250 g digestive biscuits
2 tbsps granulated sugar
4 oz/125 g butter

Crush the biscuits into very fine crumbs and mix with the sugar. Melt the butter and mix well together. Press into a large greased flan case (12 inches or 30 cm) and chill.

For the filling:
4 oz/100 g brown sugar
4 oz/100 g butter
3 eggs
6 oz/175 g golden syrup
8 oz/250 g chopped walnuts
1 lemon

Cream the butter and the sugar and beat in the eggs. Warm the syrup and beat it in thoroughly. Add the walnuts and grated lemon rind and juice. Spoon into the flan case. Cook at 350°F/180°C or gas mark 4 for 40 minutes or until puffed and golden brown. Serve cold with cream. For 6.

Walnut Bread

2 eggs
4 oz/100 g brown sugar
1 lb/500 g flour
½ tsp salt
4 tsps baking powder
1 pint/600 ml milk
6 oz/175 g chopped walnuts

Beat the eggs well and add the brown sugar. Sift the flour with the salt and baking powder, and add alternately with the milk to the egg mixture. Stir in the chopped nuts and pour into two greased bread tins. Leave to stand

for 30 minutes and then cook at 350°F/180°C or gas mark 4 for ¾ hour.
Makes two 1-lb/500-g loaves.

Pear, Orange and Walnut Jam
✷

This recipe was given to me by an American friend who lives in Burgundy
and it is one of the best and most popular jams I have ever made – indeed I
am tired of copying it out for all its admirers, so here it is for the world at
large!

>   2 oranges, washed but unpeeled
>   3 lb/1½ kg pears
>   3 lb/1½ kg sugar
>   1 lb/500 g raisins or sultanas
>   ½ cup water
>   6 oz/175 g chopped walnuts

Chop the oranges finely. Cut the pears into quarters and then slice them
crosswise. Mix with the oranges and add the sugar, raisins or sultanas, and
water. Cook, simmering gently, for 1½ hours in a heavy pan. Add the
walnuts and cook 15 minutes longer. Pot and seal. Makes five 1-lb/500-g
jars.

Brandied Walnuts
✷

Scald the walnuts with boiling water and leave to stand for 2 minutes.
Make a syrup of boiling water and sugar (2 oz/50 g sugar to 1 tablespoon
water) to thread stage (220°F/108°C).

Drain the walnuts and add to the boiling syrup. Leave to stand overnight. Drain off the syrup the next day and boil up to the thread stage
again. Pour over the walnuts and leave overnight. Repeat a third time.

The fourth day boil the syrup to strong thread stage (312°F/160°C)
and add the walnuts with an equal amount of brandy. Bring to boiling
point and pour into jars. Stored in a cool place, they will keep for several
months.

Walnut Toffee
✷

Melt 4 oz/125 g butter. Add 8 oz/250 g brown sugar and 8 oz/250 g golden syrup. Stir to hardball stage (250°F/130°C) and then add 4 oz/125 g broken walnuts.

Leave in a greased pan until nearly set, then mark into squares and leave until cold.

Pickled Walnuts

Pick the young green walnuts in July and prick them all over with a darning needle, wearing rubber gloves as you do so – otherwise your fingers will be stained brown. Put into a bowl and cover with brine made with 6 oz/175 g salt per 1 quart/1 litre water. Change the brine daily and leave for 9 days.

Remove the walnuts and put on a platter in a sunny place until they go black. Then pack into jars, cover with spiced vinegar (see page 28) and leave for 3 days. Pour off the vinegar and re-boil it hard, then pour it over the walnuts so that they are covered. Seal and store for at least 2 months before using.

Walnut Cheese

3 oz/75 g cream cheese
2 oz/50 g Cheddar cheese
a dash of Worcestershire sauce
2 oz/50 g walnut pieces

Mash the cream cheese and grate the Cheddar finely. Mix them together with a dash of Worcestershire sauce. Add two thirds of the broken walnuts and mix well. Press into a mould and cover the top with the rest of the walnuts. It makes a welcome and unusual addition to the cheese board.

Walnut and Garlic Sauce

4 oz/100 g blanched walnuts
4 cloves garlic
olive oil
salt

Grind the walnuts and pound the garlic in a mortar. Mix together and stir in the olive oil drop by drop as for mayonnaise until it reaches the consistency you require. Season to taste with salt. Serve with celery sticks or on fresh bread as a snack, or, with the addition of chopped parsley, as a sauce for pasta.

Walnut Ketchup

25 green walnuts
2 onions
2 cloves of garlic
½ oz/15 g salt
1 pint/600 ml malt vinegar
4 cloves
2 blades of mace
8 peppercorns

Chop the nuts and then pound them in a mortar until they are well crushed. Chop the onions and garlic, mix them with the nuts and add the salt and vinegar so that the nuts are well covered. Leave for 10 days, stirring regularly.

Strain off the liquid and boil it with the spices for 20 minutes. Strain and pour into bottles.

Watercress

Summer

Rorippa nasturtium-aquaticum.
Cruciferae family.

It is not safe to gather watercress from the wild – there is always a danger that it may be contaminated by sewage or industrial effluent and it can contain liver fluke. So, don't pick it; buy the cultivated watercress instead.

Wild Asparagus

Summer

Asparagus officinalis.
Liliaceae family.
Native rhizome of grasslands and cliffs.
Localized in the south west, Wales and
south-east Ireland.
Height: up to 12 inches/30 cm.
Flowers (yellow) June to August.

Asparagus is found only occasionally in the wild, particularly in Dorset, Cornwall and Gloucestershire. It can be picked, cooked and eaten in the same way as cultivated asparagus, being particularly good in sauces (mornay or mayonnaise), with *beurre noir* (see page 225), with *œufs mollets* or in croustades.

Wild Basil

Summer

Clinopodium vulgare.
Labiatae family.
Native perennial of hedgerows, wood
verges and scrub. Common except in
Scotland and Ireland.
Length: up to 2 feet/60 cm.
Flowers (pink) July to September.

Use wild basil, if you are lucky enough to find it, as a salad herb, or to flavour pasta dishes – it makes a tasty addition to macaroni cheese.

Wild Fennel

Summer

Foeniculum vulgare.
Umbelliferae family.
Native perennial found on waste ground,
verges and cliffs. Rare in Scotland and
Ireland.
Height: up to 3 feet/1 m.
Flowers (yellow) July to October.

The characteristic aniseed flavour of fennel is particularly good with fish and also in egg dishes. It makes a beautiful addition to potato soup. Well known in its cultivated form, this is a popular herb and many cookery books (see page 238) feature recipes for it.

Wild Garlic

Spring and summer

Liliaceae family.

(a) Wild Garlic or Ramsons (PLATE V)
Allium ursinum.
*Fairly common except in Scotland and
Ireland.
Height: up to 16 inches/40 cm.
Flowers (white) April to June.*

*Crow garlic (left)
Field garlic (right)*

(b) Field Garlic
Allium oleraceum
(c) Crow Garlic
Allium vineale
*Height: up to 30 inches/70 cm.
Flowers (reddish bulbils) June to August.*

The flavour of wild garlic is not so strong as that of the cultivated variety
(*Allium sativum*), especially when cooked, although all parts of the plant
smell strongly of garlic. The leaves and stalks have a very definite garlic
flavour and can be used for flavouring soups and casseroles, or chopped in
salads, or used to make garlic bread. They can be used as a garnish for
soups, as a flavouring for sauces, or in curd cheese (made as marigold

cheese on page 125, but flavoured with garlic instead of, or as well as, marigold), mixed with salt and pepper and served with oatcakes.

Wild Raspberry

Summer

Rubus idaeus.
Rosaceae family.
Found in woods and on scrubland and in
hedgerows throughout Britain.
Height: up to 60 inches/1.5 m.
Flowers May to August.
Fruits July to August.

This is the plant from which the cultivated raspberry derives and the fruits have a wonderful flavour. Eat them with caster sugar and thick cream.

Wild Strawberry

Summer

Fragaria vesca.
Rosaceae family.
Common among dry grass and in woods.
Flowers (white) April to July.
Fruits (red) June to August.

Wild strawberries have a beautiful flavour and are much sought after by gourmets as a great delicacy, especially in France. An infusion made from the leaves gives a tea that is as fragrant as China tea.

Wild Strawberry Flan
❦

Line a greased 8-inch/20-cm flan dish with sweet crust pastry and bake it blind.

Soak enough wild strawberries to fill the case in white wine with a little sugar, until they are soft. Lift out with a slotted spoon and put into the flan case. Heat the wine mixture gently so that all the sugar is dissolved and then stir in a little gelatine, previously soaked in a little of the liquid. Cool. Pour over the strawberries and leave to set. Serve with thick cream.

Wild Strawberries in Syrup
❦

2 lb/1 kg wild strawberries
12 oz/325 g sugar

Put the strawberries in a bowl and sprinkle with a little of the sugar. Leave to stand overnight. Then drain off the liquid and add to the rest of the sugar. Dissolve over a low heat, then boil rapidly to make a syrup. After 10 minutes, add the strawberries and cook for a few minutes longer. Pour into small hot jars and cover. It stores for 2 or 3 weeks.

Wild Strawberry Jam

Sprinkle wild strawberries with sugar and leave to stand overnight. Next day, pour off the juices into a small pan and boil for 1 minute, stirring all the time. Add the berries and simmer, with more sugar to taste and a little lemon juice, for 30 minutes. Pot in very small jars. Don't over-cook it – it never sets very hard. Eat within 2 or 3 weeks.

Wild Strawberry Jelly

2 lb/1 kg wild strawberries
juice of 1 lemon
1 pint/600 ml water
sugar

Put the strawberries in a pan with the lemon juice and water. Bring to the boil and simmer for 10 minutes. Strain through a jelly-bag and measure the juice. Add $\frac{3}{4}$ lb/325 g sugar to every 1 pint/600 ml and dissolve over a low heat. Cook briskly to setting point. Pot and seal.

Wild strawberries are a mouth-watering addition to cloudberry sorbet (see page 46), and they also feature in the exotic dessert below which is so extravagantly decadent that I had to include it – if for no other reason than its entire concept is in such contrast to that of hedgerow cookery! It comes from one of the most famous restaurants in France.

Le Grand Dessert Troisgros

1 pint/600 ml vanilla ice cream
$\frac{1}{2}$ pint/300 ml strawberry sorbet
10 oz/300 g strawberries
10 oz/300 g wild strawberries
10 oz/300 g raspberries (wild if possible)
12 plums
1 lb/500 g each pears and peaches,
    poached in syrup (see page 37)
    and flavoured with vanilla

        raspberry syrup (from wild raspberry
          jam, made as wild strawberry jam
          opposite)
        double cream

Place the vanilla ice cream in the centre of a shallow round dish and crown it with the sorbet. Arrange the fruits around the outside and pour the syrup over the top. Pipe the outer edges of the plate with whipped cream and serve with *petits fours*.

As the finishing touch, perhaps this should be followed by the recipe below.

Sir Walter Raleigh's Cordial
✧

'Take a gallon of strawberries, and put into them a pinte of aqua vitae, let them stand four or five dayes, strain them gently out, and sweeten the water as you please with fine sugar, or else perfume.' (Perhaps he had rose water in mind.)

W.M. (cook to Queen Henrietta Maria),
The Queen's Closet Opened, 1655

Wood Sorrel

Summer

Oxalis acetosella.
Oxalidaceae family.
Native perennial of woods and hedgerows,
throughout Britain.
Height: up to 6 inches/15 cm.
Flowers (white) April to June.

Very similar in taste to sorrel (see page 185), this little plant has leaves which are particularly good, raw, in salads. They can be used in all the recipes given for sorrel.

Yarrow <small>(PLATE VII)</small>

(*Milfoil*)

Summer

Achillea millefolium.
Compositae family.
Native perennial, very common on road
verges, in meadows, hedgerows and
gardens.
Height: up to 18 inches/45 cm.
Flowers (pink with white and purple)
June to November.

Achilles is reputed to have applied yarrow to wounds inflicted with iron weapons, and in Anglo-Saxon folklore it was thought to be a potent protection against evil. Sometimes it used to be taken as snuff, and derived a local name of 'old man's pepper'. The leaves, which have quite a strong taste, can be added to salads, used in herb bread (see page 89), or made into tea (see page 196). They can also be cooked as a vegetable. Boil the younger leaf stems in salted water until tender, then drain and chop them and simmer in a little butter for a few minutes longer. Alternatively, add to a little béchamel sauce.

Yarrow Salad

Wash and chop equal quantities of yarrow, plantain and watercress. Chop $\frac{1}{2}$ a cucumber, 1 cold potato and some chives and parsley. Toss all together in a garlicky vinaigrette.

Yellow Archangel

Summer

Lamiastrum galeobdolon.
Labiatae family.
Native perennial of woods and clearings
in southern England and the Midlands.
Height: up to 18 inches/50 cm.
Flowers (yellow) May to June.

The leaves of yellow archangel can be used in the same ways as chickweed.

Yellow Rocket (PLATE VII)

(Landcress, Wintercress)

Most of the year round

Barbarea vulgaris.
Cruciferae family.
Native biennial or perennial, fairly
common except in northern Scotland.
Found in damp hedgerows and on road
verges.
Height: up to 3 feet/80 cm.
Flowers (yellow) May to September.

This plant leafs throughout the winter and is often used to flavour salads in Italy, where it is known as *rucola* or *ruchetta*. It has a strong, deliciously spicy taste and mixes very well with other saladings.

Its generic name is said to be after St Barbara, whose saint's day is on 4 December when wintercress is in abundant leaf.

Rocket Salad

This recipe is as described enthusiastically by a friend – I haven't tried it yet myself but it sounds marvellous.

Mix some tiny, fresh, undercooked broad beans with rocket leaves and purslane leaves and dress with a good vinaigrette.

Making Wines from Hedgerow Plants

I am attempting here only to give a basic outline of the processes and method of wine-making for those who would like to try their hand at it for the first time. There are many excellent books on home wine-making for those who wish to explore the subject thoroughly (see Bibliography on page 238).

When yeast and sugar are dissolved in water, at the right temperature, fermentation takes place. The Latin word *fermentare* means 'to cause to rise', and the name was given to the bubbling process by Pasteur to describe an enzymatic reaction where the yeast acting on the sugar produces alcohol and releases carbon dioxide gas which gives the appearance of boiling.

In wine-making, the minimum amount of sugar to 1 gallon/4 litres of water is 2 lb 6 oz/1 kg. If you add more sugar than this, the wine will be a correspondingly sweeter one, since not all the sugar will be used up by the fermentation process. The addition of lemons improves the flavour of the wine and provides citric acid in cases where natural acidity is lacking; or else you can use citric acid, which is available at most chemists. Another useful additive is tannin – it helps to clear the wine, particularly flower wines: just add a cupful of cold tea to the brew. For the beginner, fresh or dried baker's yeast makes for perfectly satisfactory results. The best temperature for fermentation is about 70 to 75°F/21 to 24°C, so a place next to the boiler, or in an airing cupboard, is ideal. It is important to ensure warmth to get it going, and also not to vary the temperature of the place where the wine is fermenting after it has started.

The golden rule of home wine-making is cleanliness: it is of paramount importance to the success of the wine. The vinegar bug, *Mycoderma aceti*, must be kept out at all costs during the fermentation process, and this is achieved by inserting an airlock. All equipment must be washed, rinsed and sterilized so as not to infect the ingredients, and you can do this by using a sterilizing solution made up of 1 crushed Campden tablet and 1 teaspoon of lemon juice dissolved in ½ pint/300 ml water. You can re-use this solution a number of times. Never use anything metallic in the brewing process.

On the whole, it's not worth making less than 1 gallon/4 litres at a time, considering the amount of care and work that goes into producing a good wine.

Essential Equipment

1. A sterile, lidded polythene bucket or dustbin-type container.
2. A strainer (cloth or nylon).
3. A sterilized bottle for stirring and crushing the ingredients.
4. Clean 1-gallon/4-litre or 2-gallon/8-litre fermentation jars, preferably glass.
5. A fermentation airlock with cork.
6. A syphon tube, rubber or polythene, about $\frac{1}{4}$ inch/$\frac{1}{2}$ cm in diameter.
7. Campden tablets.
8. Wine bottles and new corks.
9. A wine rack.

Method

For All Wines

Pick the flowers or fruits on a sunny day when they are not overblown or overripe. Remove all stalks and leaves, and the calyces and sheaths from the flowers. Wash the fruits well, and dip flowers into sterilizing solution (see above).

For Wines Made with Berries and Fruits

1. Put the washed fruits – and chopped raisins and sultanas where indicated – into a sterilized bucket or container. Stone the large fruits, such as bullaces, etc., and chop them.
2. Pour boiling water over them and leave to stand, well-covered, stirring occasionally and pressing the ingredients with a sterilized bottle to extract the juices. For every 1 gallon/4 litres wine you need to pour 2 quarts/2 litres over the fruit. Leave to stand, well-covered, for 24 hours.

3. Mix the yeast with 2 teaspoons sugar and ¼ pint/150 ml of the liquid, heated to 75°F/24°C. When it starts to ferment, add it to the mixture with the juice and rind of lemon or orange, or some citric acid, and half the sugar dissolved in 1 quart/1 litre boiling water. The fermenting yeast mixture should not be added to the sugar solution until it is at 75°F/24°C or a little below, otherwise it may kill the yeast. This mixture is called the 'must'. Leave it to ferment on the pulp for the specified number of days: the shorter the pulp fermentation, the quicker the wine will mature.

4. Strain into a fermentation jar, add the rest of the sugar, so that the jar is two thirds full, and shake well. Insert an airlock containing some sterilizing solution (see above). Fermentation will often be fierce with baker's yeast, so keep an eye on the jar in case the wine overflows through the airlock.

5. Put it in a warm place (about 70°F/21°C) to ferment to a finish. You will be able to tell when the fermentation has ceased by the fact that there is no more bubbling in the airlock, even when you have given the jar a shake. It will take anything from 2 to 4 months to finish fermenting. Sediment will have gone to the bottom and there may be little bits of matter floating around in the wine.

6. Syphon off into another jar of the same size, leaving the sediment untouched. (This is called 'racking'.) Top up with water and then cork securely and leave for 3 months in a cool place. You may have to rack your wine a number of times before it is really clear.

7. Syphon off into sterilized bottles and cork down. Always leave your wines for 6 months before drinking – you will probably find that they are better if left for a year or longer. Store them at an even, cool temperature in wine racks. They should be kept on their sides to keep the corks moist: if they dry out and shrink they will fail to seal the bottle and the wine will be spoiled.

For Flower Wines

In this method the flowers are not allowed to come into contact with hot water, therefore a 'must' is prepared before the addition of the flowers. This is made with sultanas or raisins and the flowers are added after the original fermentation has taken place.

To every 2 quarts/2 litres of flower heads (except in the cases of rose petals and elderflowers, when fewer flowers are needed), make a must with: 8 oz/250 g sultanas or raisins, 1 quart/1 litre water, juice of 1 lemon (or more where specified), 2½ lb/1¼ kg sugar, 1 tsp yeast. (This will be sufficient for 1 gallon/4 litres wine.)

1. Wash and mince the sultanas or raisins and put them in a sterilized plastic bowl.

2. Cover with boiling water and add the lemon juice and half the sugar. Stir until the sugar has dissolved.

3. Over a pan of boiling water, heat the mixture to fermentation heat (75°F/24°C) and add the yeast mixed with a little of the hot liquid and let it start to ferment. Stir it in well and cover the bowl. Ferment for about a week, stirring several times a day with a sterilized bottle (see above).

4. Add the flowers to the must and stir them, crushing them as you do so. Ferment in the bowl for a further 5 days and then strain into a fermentation jar.

5. Dissolve the remaining sugar in another 1 quart/1 litre of hot water and, when it has cooled, pour it into the jar to make it two thirds full (see note 4 on page 222). Continue to make the wine as 'For Wines Made with Berries and Fruits', notes 5 to 7 above.

Some Basic Recipes

Béchamel Sauce

1½ oz/40 g butter
2 tbsps flour
½ pint/300 ml heated milk
salt and pepper

Melt the butter in a thick-bottomed saucepan. Gradually stir in the flour with a wooden spoon, then add the milk slowly, stirring all the time until the sauce thickens. Season to taste. Simmer very gently over a low heat for 10 minutes.

To reheat, put over a pan of simmering water. For certain dishes which require a different type of sauce, you can use stock instead of milk.

For *sauce à la crème*, add double cream to the finished béchamel, or, in special cases, use single cream instead of milk.

Oil Pastry

For two 8-inch/20-cm flan dishes:

10 oz/300 g plain flour
½ tsp salt
¼ pint/150 ml vegetable oil
3 tbsps water

Sieve the flour, add the salt and mix in the oil and the water. Stir well together and knead briefly until smooth. Press around the oiled pie dish with your knuckles and bake immediately. Do not chill or roll out.

To bake blind

Press the pastry into the oiled flan dish and trim around the edge. Line the pastry shell with foil and fill with baking beans. Cook at 350°F/180°C or gas mark 4 for 15 to 20 minutes. Remove the foil for the last few minutes of cooking. Cool on a wire rack. (Alternatively, prick the pastry all over with a fork and bake without either foil or beans.)

Pancake Batter

❦

For 18–20 pancakes:

¾ pint/450 ml cold water and milk,
   mixed
4 eggs
¼ tsp salt
8 oz/250 g sifted flour
4 tbsps melted butter

Liquidize the water and milk with the eggs and salt. Then add the flour
and the butter. Blend for 1 minute. Cover and chill for 2 hours. Make the
pancakes in the usual way.

Beurre Noir

❦

For each helping: 1 oz/25 g butter and 1 tablespoon vinegar. Cut the butter
into pieces and heat it gently. As it gets very hot it will foam and froth and
then turn golden brown. Pour in the vinegar and let the mixture sizzle and
rage around for a minute or so. Season as necessary with salt and pepper
and keep over hot water until ready to serve. For the best *beurre noir*, use
clarified butter (see below).

Clarified Butter

❦

Cut the butter into pieces and melt it over a moderate heat. Leave it to
settle for a few moments, skim off the white foam and then strain the clear
yellow part of the butter through muslin into a bowl, leaving the milky
residue in the bottom of the pan.

Jam-Making

❦

Testing without a Thermometer

To establish setting point, remove the jam from the heat and put a
teaspoonful in a cold saucer. Allow to cool. If setting point has been
reached, the surface will set and the jam remain divided when pushed
apart with the finger.

Testing with a Thermometer

Put the thermometer into the jam during the early part of the cooking. Setting point is reached for most jams at 220°F/110°C. Allow the thermometer to cool before you rinse it clean.

Volume Guide

3 lb/1.5 kg sugar used in a recipe will render 5 lb/2.5 kg jam.

To Pot and Seal

Cover the cooled jam with a round of waxed paper, and put a piece of plastic film over the jar, holding it either with a rubber band or with a screw-top lid.

Notes on Storing

Preserves

Food preserved in vinegar will keep indefinitely if stored in clean screw-top jars and kept airtight, but is best eaten within 18 months.

Candied Flowers

If completely coated with the sugar solution and stored in clean airtight jars, these will store for up to a year.

Edible Wild Plants and Their Seasons

The time when a plant is at its best for the purposes of cooking varies quite considerably according to the weather conditions of the year in question, and of course there is also a marked variation in season between those plants that grow further north and those that are found in the more clement south of Britain. So the list here just gives a general idea of season.

SPRING

Alexanders
Alfalfa
Beech
Bellflower
Birch
Bistort
Broom
Butcher's broom
Chickweed
Comfrey
Corn salad
Cowslip
Crab-apple
Dandelion
Dock
Douglas fir

Elder
Elm
Garlic mustard
Golden saxifrage
Goosegrass
Hawthorn
Hop
Lady's mantle
Lady's smock
Mushrooms
Nettle
Parsley piert
Pine
Primrose
Violet
Wild garlic

SUMMER

Angelica
Ash
Basil-thyme
Bittercresses
Borage
Burdock

Chamomile
Chickweed
Chicory
Chive
Clary
Comfrey

SUMMER *(continued)*

Corn salad
Cow parsley
Dandelion
Deadnettle
Dock
Douglas fir
Elder
Fat hen
Garlic mustard
Good King Henry
Goosegrass
Ground elder
Hogweed
Horseradish
Japonica
Lady's mantle
Lime
Mallow
Marigold
Marjoram
Marsh samphire
Marsh thistle
Meadowsweet
Mint
Mushrooms
Nasturtium
Nettle
Oak
Orache
Parsley piert

Pine
Plantain
Purslane
Rock samphire
Rose petals
Salad burnet
Seabeet
Seakale
Sea purslane
Seaweeds
Shepherd's purse
Sorrel
Sow thistle
Sweet cicely
Tansy
Thyme
Wall lettuce
Walnut (green)
Watercress
Wild asparagus
Wild basil
Wild fennel
Wild garlics
Wild raspberry
Wild strawberry
Wood sorrel
Yarrow
Yellow archangel
Yellow rocket

AUTUMN

Barberry
Bilberry
Blackberry
Bullace
Cherry
Chestnut
Chickweed
Cloudberry
Cob-nut
Corn salad
Cowberry
Crab-apple
Cranberry
Dewberry

Elder
Guelder rose
Hawthorn
Juniper
Medlar
Mushrooms
Oak
Rose
Rowan
Sloe
Snowberry
Walnut
Yellow rocket

Protected Plants of the British Isles

Alpine gentian (*Gentiana nivalis*)
Alpine sow-thistle (*Cicerbita alpina*)
Alpine woodsia (*Woodsia alpina*)
Blue heath (*Phyllodoce caerulea*)
Cheddar pink (*Dianthus gratianopolitanus*)
Diapensia (*Diapensia lapponica*)
Drooping saxifrage (*Saxifraga cernua*)
Ghost orchid (*Epipogium aphyllum*)
Killarney fern (*Trichomanes speciosum*)
Lady's slipper (*Cypripedium calceolus*)
Mezereon (*Daphne mezereum*)
Military orchid (*Orchis militaris*)
Monkey orchid (*Orchis simia*)
Oblong woodsia (*Woodsia ilvensis*)
Red helleborine (*Cephalanthera rubra*)
Snowden lily (*Lloydia serotina*)
Spiked speedwell (*Veronica spicata*)
Spring gentian (*Gentiana verna*)
Teesdale sandwort (*Minuartia stricta*)
Tufted saxifrage (*Saxifraga cespitosa*)
Wild gladiolus (*Gladiolus illyricus*)

Information about how to join the Botanical Society of the British Isles can be obtained from:

> The Hon. General Secretary, Botanical Society of the British Isles, c/o Department of Botany, Natural History Museum, Cromwell Road, London SW7 5BP.

Poisonous Plants

Alder buckthorn (*Frangula alnus*)
Baneberry (*Actaea spicata*)
Bittersweet or woody nightshade (*Solanum dulcamara*)
Black bryony (*Tamus communis*)
Black nightshade (*Solanum nigrum*)
Buttercup (*Ranunculus*) – all species
Columbine (*Aquilegia vulgaris*)
Common buckthorn (*Rhamnus cathartica*)
Cow bane (*Cicuta virosa*)
Darnel rye grass (*Lolium temulentum*)
Deadly nightshade (*Atropa belladonna*)
Dog's mercury (*Mercurialis perennis*)
Fine-leaved water dropwort (*Oenanthe aquatica*)
Fool's parsley (*Aethusa cynapium*)
Foxglove (*Digitalis purpurea*)
Fritillary (*Fritillaria meleagris*)
Green hellebore (*Helleborus viridis*)
Hemlock (*Conium maculatum*)
Hemlock water dropwort (*Oenanthe crocata*)
Henbane (*Hyoscyamus niger*)
Ivy (*Hedera helix*)
Lily of the valley (*Convallaria majalis*)
Lords and ladies (*Arum maculatum*)
Meadow saffron (*Colchium autumnale*)
Mezereon (*Daphne mezereum*)
Mistletoe (*Viscum album*)
Monkshood (*Aconitum anglicum*)
Privet (*Ligustrum vulgare*)
Spindle tree (*Euonymus europaeus*)
Spurge (*Euphorbia*) – all species
Spurge-laurel (*Daphne laureola*)

Stinking hellebore (*Helleborus foetidus*)
Thorn apple (*Datura stramonium*)
Tubular water dropwort (*Oenanthe fistulosa*)
White bryony (*Bryonia dioica*)
Yew (*Taxus baccata*)

Dangerous Plants, or Plants to be Avoided

Acrid lobelia (*Lobelia urens*)
Anemone or windflower – all species
Animal mercury (*Mercurialis annua*)
Bluebell (*Endymion nonscriptus*)
Bog asphodel (*Narthecium ossifragum*)
Box (*Buxus sempervirens*)
Bracken – all species
Broomrape (*Orobanche* spp.)
Bryony or white bryony (*Bryonia dioica*)
Buckwheat (*Polygonum fagopyrum*)
Castor oil plant (*Ricinus communis*)
Charlock or wild mustard (*Sinapis arvensis*)
Common flax (*Linum usitatissimum*)
Common or scarlet pimpernel (*Anagallis arvensis*)
Common rhododendron (*Rhododendron ponticum*)
Common storksbill (*Erodium cicutarium*)
Common vetch (*Vicia sativa*)
Corn cockle (*Agrostemma gigatho*)
Crowfoot (*Ranunculus sceleratus* and *R. acris*)
Delphinium – all species
Everlasting pea (*Lathyrus sylvestris*)
Fodder beet, sugar beet or mangels (*Beta vulgaris cicla*)
Grass vetchling (*Lathyrus nissolia*)
Greater celandine (*Chelidonium magus*)
Great spearwort (*Ranunculus lingua*)
Groundnut, earthnut or monkey nut (*Arachis hypogeaea*)
Hairy medick (*Medicago polymorpha*)
Hairy vetchling (*Lathyrus hirsutus*)
Heliotrope (*Heliotropum europaeum*)
Hemp or marijuana species (Cannabiaceae)
Herb Paris (*Paris quadrifolia*)

Horned poppy or sea poppy (*Glaucium flavum*)
Hound's tongue (*Cynoglossum officinale*)
Hyacinth – all species
Indian or nutter pea (*Lathyrus sativus*)
Knotweed, knotgrass or wireweed (*Polygonum hydropiper*)
Laburnum (*Cytisus laburnum*)
Large dodder (*Ciscuta europaea*)
Lesser celandine (*Ranunculus ficaria*)
Lesser spearwort (*Ranunculus flammula*)
Lupin – all species
Marsh arrow grass (*Triglochin palustris*)
Marsh marigold or kingcup (*Caltha palustris*)
Meadow rue (*Thalictrum*)
Persicaria or peachwort (*Polygonum persicaria*)
Pheasant's eye (*Adonis annua*)
Pokeweed or pigeonberry (*Phytolacca americana*)
Purging flax (*Linum catharicum*)
Purple viper's bugloss (*Echium lycopsis*)
Rape (*Brassica napus*)
Red poppy (*Papaverum rhoeas*)
Rhubarb leaves (*Rheum rhaponticum*)
St John's wort (*Hypericum* spp.)
Sea arrow grass (*Triglochin maritima*)
Sedum species
Soapwort or hedge pink (*Saponaria officinalis*)
Sowbread or common cyclamen (*Cyclamen hederifolium*)
Stinking iris or roast beef plant (*Iris foetidissima*)
Thyme-leaved sandwort (*Arenaria serpyllifolia*)
Tobacco plant (*Nicotiana tabacum*)
Traveller's joy or old man's beard (*Clematis vitalba*)
Water figwort (*Scrophularia aquatica*)
Water parsnip (*Sium latifolium*)
Water pepper or smartweed (*Polygonum hydropiper*)
White mustard (*Sinapis alba*)
White or opium poppy (*Papaver somniferum*)
Yellow flag or yellow iris (*Iris pseudocorus*)

Plant Families

Berberidaceae (barberry)

Betulaceae (birch)

Boraginaceae (borage, comfrey)

Campanulaceae (bellflower)

Cannabiaceae (hop)

Caprifoliaceae (elder, guelder rose, snowberry)

Caryophyllaceae (chickweed)

Chenopodiaceae (fat hen, good king henry, orache, marsh samphire, seabeet, sea purslane)

Compositae (burdock, chamomile, chicory, dandelion, marigold, marsh thistle, sow thistle, tansy, wall lettuce, yarrow)

Corylaceae (cob-nut)

Cruciferae (bittercress, garlic mustard, horseradish, lady's smock, nasturtium, seakale, shepherd's purse, watercress, yellow rocket)

Cupressaceae (juniper)

Ericaceae (bilberry, cowberry, cranberry)

Fagaceae (beech, oak, sweet chestnut)

Gigartinaceae (carragheen)

Labiatae (basil-thyme, clary, deadnettle, marjoram, mint, thyme, wild basil, yellow archangel)

Juglandaceae (walnut)

Leguminosae (alfalfa, broom)

Liliaceae (butcher's broom, chives, wild asparagus, wild garlic)

Malvaceae (mallow)

Oleaceae (ash)

Oxalidaceae (wood sorrel)

Pinaceae (Douglas fir, pine)

Plantaginaceae (plantain)

Polygonaceae (bistort, dock, sorrel)

Portulaceae (purslane)

Primulaceae (cowslip, primrose)

Rhodophyllaceae (laver)

Rosaceae (blackberry, bullace, cherry, cloudberry, crab-apple, dewberry, hawthorn, japonica, lady's mantle, meadowsweet, medlar, parsley piert, roses, rowan, salad burnet, sloe, wild raspberry, wild strawberry)

Rubiaceae (goosegrass)

Saxifragaceae (golden saxifrage)

Tiliaceae (lime)

Tropaeolaceae (nasturtium)

Ulmaceae (elm)

Umbelliferae (alexanders, angelica, cow parsley, ground elder, hogweed, rock samphire, sweet cicely, wild celery, wild fennel)

Urticaceae (nettle)

Valerianaceae (corn salad)

Violaceae (violet)

Bibliography

Baker, Margaret, *Discovering the Folklore of Plants*, Shire, 1969

Beedell, Suzanne, *Pick, Cook and Brew*, Pelham Books, 1973

The Diary of a Farmer's Wife 1796–1797, Countrywise Books, 1964

Gerard: *Leaves from Gerard's Herball*, arranged by Marcus Woodward, Dover, 1969

Grieve, Mrs M., *A Modern Herbal*, Penguin, 1976

Grigson, Geoffrey, *The Englishman's Flora*, Paladin, 1975

Hyde, Molly, *Hedgerow Plants*, Shire Publications, 1975

Johnson, Hugh, *The International Book of Trees*, Mitchell Beazley, 1973

Joice, Jean, *Some Bygone Garden Herbs and Plants*, BBC Anglia, 1977

Keble Martin, W., *The Concise British Flora in Colour*, Michael Joseph, 1965

Mabey, Richard, *Food for Free*, Fontana/Collins, 1975/2

Phillips, Roger, *Wild Flowers of Britain*, Pan and Ward Lock, 1977

    Trees in Britain, Pan and Ward Lock, 1978

Stobart, Tom, *Herbs, Spices and Flavourings*, Penguin, 1977

Wynne Hatfield, Audrey, *How to Enjoy Your Weeds*, Muller, 1969

Books Recommended for Mushrooms

Grigson, Jane, *Good Things*, Penguin, 1973

    The Mushroom Feast, Penguin, 1978

Hvass, E. and H., *Mushrooms and Toadstools in Colour*, Blandford, 1961

Lange, M., and Hora, F.B., *Collins Guide to Mushrooms and Toadstools*, Collins, 1963

Montagné, Prosper, *Larousse Gastronomique*, Hamlyn, 1961

Nilsson, S., and Persson, O., *Fungi of Northern Europe*, (Penguin Nature Guides) Penguin, 1978

The Oxford Book of Food Plants, Oxford University Press, 1969

Tosco, Uberto, *The World of Mushrooms*, Orbis, 1973

Tribe, Ian (ed.), *Mushrooms in the Wild*, Orbis, 1977

Books Recommended for Herb Cookery

Grieve, Mrs M., *A Modern Herbal*, Penguin, 1976

Hemphill, Rosemary, *The Penguin Book of Herbs and Spices*, Penguin, 1966

   Herbs for All Seasons, Penguin, 1975

Loewenfeld, C., and Beck, P., *Herbs for Health and Cookery*, Pan, 1965

Books Recommended for Wine-Making

Bravery, *Complete Book of Home Wine-Making*, Pan, 1973

Johnson, Hugh, *World Atlas of Wine*, Mitchell Beazley, 1971

Mitchell, *Scientific Winemaking Made Easy*, Amateur Winemaker, 1969

Tayleur, W.H.T., *Penguin Book of Home Brewing and Wine Making*, Penguin, 1973

Turner, Ben, *The Compleat Home Wine-Maker and Brewer*, Emblem, 1976

Wicks, Keith, *Wine and Wine-Making*, Macdonald Educational, 1976

Wise, Dorothy (compiler), *Home Made Country Wines*, Hamlyn, 1971

Cookbooks

Hartley, Dorothy, *Food in England*, Macdonald & Jane's, 1964

Mabey, David and Rose, *Jams, Pickles and Chutneys*, Penguin, 1976

White, Florence, *Good Things in England*, Cape, 1932, and Futura, 1974

Reference Books for Poisonous and Dangerous Plants

Forsyth, A.A., *British Poisonous Plants*, H.M.S.O., 1968

North, Pamela, *Poisonous Plants and Fungi in Colour*, Blandford Press, 1967

Tampion, John, *Dangerous Plants*, David & Charles, 1977

Weights and Measures

Solid Measures

Approximate equivalents:

British	Metric	Metric	British
1 lb (16 oz)	500 g	1 kilo (1000 g)	2 lb
½ lb (8 oz)	250 g	½ kilo (500 g)	1 lb
¼ lb (4 oz)	100–125 g	¼ kilo (250 g)	8 oz
1 oz	25 g	100 g	4 oz

Liquid Measures

British

1 quart	= 2 pints	= 40 fl oz
1 pint		= 20 fl oz
½ pint	= 1 cup	= 10 fl oz
¼ pint	= 8 tablespoons	= 5 fl oz
	1 tablespoon	= ½ fl oz (just over)
	1 dessertspoon	= ⅓ fl oz
	1 teaspoon	= ⅙ fl oz

Metric

1 litre = 10 decilitres (dl) = 100 centilitres (cl) = 1000 millilitres (ml)

Approximate equivalents:

British	Metric	Metric	British
1 quart	1.1 litre	1 litre	35 fl oz
1 pint	600 ml	½ litre (500 ml)	18 fl oz
½ pint	300 ml	¼ litre (250 ml)	9 fl oz
¼ pint	150 ml	100 ml	4 fl oz
1 tablespoon	15 ml		
1 dessertspoon	10 ml		
1 teaspoon	5 ml		

American

1 quart	=	2 pints	= 32 fl oz
1 pint	=	2 cups	= 16 fl oz
		1 cup	= 8 fl oz
		1 tablespoon	= $\frac{1}{3}$ fl oz
		1 teaspoon	= $\frac{1}{6}$ fl oz

Approximate equivalents:

British	American	American	British
1 quart	2$\frac{1}{2}$ pints	1 quart	1$\frac{1}{2}$ pints + 3 tbsps (32 fl oz)
1 pint	1$\frac{1}{4}$ pints	1 pint	$\frac{3}{4}$ pint + 2 tbsps (16 fl oz)
$\frac{1}{2}$ pint	10 fl oz (1$\frac{1}{4}$ cups)	1 cup	$\frac{1}{2}$ pint − 2 tbsps (8 fl oz)
$\frac{1}{4}$ pint	5 fl oz		
1 tablespoon	1$\frac{1}{2}$ tablespoons		
1 dessertspoon	1 tablespoon		
1 teaspoon	$\frac{1}{3}$ fl oz		

Temperature Equivalents for Oven Thermostat Markings

Fahrenheit	Gas Mark	Centigrade	Heat of Oven
225°	$\frac{1}{4}$	110°	Very cool
250°	$\frac{1}{2}$	120–130°	Very cool
275°	1	140°	Cool
300°	2	150°	Cool
325°	3	160–170°	Moderate
350°	4	180°	Moderate
375°	5	190°	Fairly hot
400°	6	200°	Fairly hot
425°	7	220°	Hot
450°	8	230°	Very hot
475°	9	240°	Very hot

Index

More About Penguins
and Pelicans

Penguinews, which appears every month, contains details of all the new books issued by Penguins as they are published. It is supplemented by our stocklist, which includes almost 5,000 titles.

A specimen copy of *Penguinews* will be sent to you free on request. Please write to Dept EP, Penguin Books Ltd, Harmondsworth, Middlesex, for your copy.

In the U.S.A.: For a complete list of books available from Penguins in the United States write to Dept CS, Penguin Books, 625 Madison Avenue, New York, New York 10022.

In Canada: For a complete list of books available from Penguins in Canada write to Penguin Books Canada Ltd, 2801 John Street, Markham Ontario L3R 1B4.

In Australia: For a complete list of books available from Penguins in Australia write to the Marketing Department, Penguin Books Australia Ltd, P.O. Box 257, Ringwood, Victoria 3134.

Penguin Handbooks offer an enormous range of practical guides to help you with cooking, drinking, sewing, knitting, gardening, sports, hobbies, child care, the law – all these and many more. Some of them are listed on the following pages.

Cookery and Wine

THE FARMHOUSE KITCHEN
Mary Norwak

A bevy of recipes, with notes on their history, which includes all the traditional country occupations of bread-making, pickling and brewing as well as delicious and time-honoured meals.

VEGETABLE COOKERY
Nika Hazelton

An A-Z of vegetables, both fresh and dried, with their history, ways of keeping and preserving them, their nutritional value, and a host of exciting recipes.

LEAVE IT TO COOK
Stella Attenbury

Slow cooking makes food taste better and saves time. Here are recipes for meat, fish, soups, casseroles, vegetables, sweets and savouries that you can leave for up to eight hours and only improve the taste.

HERBS FOR ALL SEASONS
Rosemary Hemphill

In four parts, one for each season, this book gives instructions for planting, growing and drying each plant, with a variety of recipes to suit all tastes and a fascinating collection of herbal remedies and beauty aids.

Gardening

THE WELL-TEMPERED GARDEN
Christopher Lloyd

'I cannot remember when I enjoyed a book so much, and no matter what your special interests may be, I cannot recommend it too highly – Ron Hay in *The Times*

THE PIP BOOK
Keith Mossman

'The perfect present for the young enthusiast, *The Pip Book* should ensure that even the most reluctant avocado puts down roots and sends up shoots' – *The Times*

ORGANIC GARDENING
Lawrence D. Hills

The author gives detailed instruction for growing a wide range of fruits and vegetables by organic principles, many of them varieties no longer available from shops.

TOWN GARDENS TO LIVE IN
Susan Jellicoe and Marjory Allen

Here is a book about creating the kind of garden *you* want to live in: formal, naturalistic, or just plain easy to keep.

THE NEW VEGETABLE GROWER'S HANDBOOK
Arthur J. Simons

Practical and exact instruction combined with sound scientific explanation make this one of the most reliable 'green-finger' manuals on sale.